GREEN ZONE DIARY

A Diplomat's War Story

Dear Ebony—
thank you for
Supporting women's
values!

Amy Madsen

A M Y   M A D S E N

Green Zone Diary
©2021, Amy Madsen

ISBN: 978-1-09836-244-7
ISBN eBook: 978-1-09836-245-4

For all State Department Employees who have, or are serving, in war zones.

A portion of the sales of *Green Zone Diary* will go to *Undivided: Women War &*
The Battle for Peace. Undivided is a storytelling platform to create community and
empower women in conflict zones. To learn more about Undivided, go to
www.womenundivided.org

CONTENTS

PREFACE

In 2005, I moved to Baghdad, Iraq, as an employee of the U.S. Department of State. I spent one year working and living in a war zone. While there, I met many strong, resilient, and highly capable Iraqi women. Humbled by their life experiences, I vowed that someday, somehow, I was going to share their stories and those of strong, capable women like them, who are working around the world to advance peace and make a positive difference for future generations.

Fifteen years and hundreds of conversations later, I cofounded a nonprofit organization, Undivided: Women, War & The Battle for Peace. Undivided is focused on creating community and empowering women in crisis zones through storytelling. I firmly believe that by recognizing women's roles in conflict, we can elevate their voices in creating peace.

While promoting Undivided and talking to women who have lived through war and conflict, I've found 100 percent support the concept of our organization. There's a smaller percentage that are actually willing to share their stories. Some are understandably unable to relive their trauma. Others feel their voice is not important because they know women who "had it worse" or "suffered more." This feeling, that their voices or stories are not important enough to share, is one I completely understand. For years, I thought my own story didn't matter. I could have had it worse, much worse. I could have been in the U.S. Military and been sent to the frontlines, instead of being protected in Baghdad's Green Zone. I could have been a local woman, losing my family and friends, helplessly watching my country fall apart. But I wasn't either of those things.

Listening to women tell me their voices didn't matter finally made me realize I needed to do the very thing I was asking them to do. I had to share my own story—regardless of how I felt, regardless of how vulnerable it would make me, regardless of how I might be judged. And so, in the middle of the COVID-19 pandemic, I sat at my desk and completed my war story. Some days, I would walk away from my writing in frustration, unable to capture the nuance of my thoughts. Other days, I would pound away on my laptop, as if possessed, tears actively dripping down my cheeks.

Green Zone Diary: A Diplomat's War Story is the result. Different from the military accounts depicted in films and read about in books and articles, it chronicles the perspective of one civilian, very junior, State Department official who served in Iraq, whose mundane bureaucratic tasks were all too often interrupted by the tragedy of war.

CHAPTER 1:

And So It Began

My boss handed me a thin manila file. Glancing at it briefly, I saw no markings or labels indicating its purpose. And by testing its weight in my hand, I guessed it contained only a few loose sheets of paper. It was my first day on the job, and it had been less than twelve hours since I'd arrived in Baghdad's Green Zone. After briefly welcoming me to Iraq and introducing me to my colleagues for the next year, my boss gave me my first task for the day. As the newly appointed American Citizen Services Officer, it was my job to call a wife whose husband had been blown up by a bomb—on the side of the road, a day or two before. All the information I needed, she said as she lightly tapped the folder with her fingertips, was contained in that one, thin manila folder.

I froze, momentarily standing there, my mouth agape for what felt like at least a minute. In reality, it was probably more like two seconds.

And then, much like a heater furiously whirring to life on a cold winter morning, my brain kicked in and went straight to high gear. I had one of those disconnected moments where what I was actually thinking on the inside highly differed from what I was expressing on the outside. Internally, my hands were frantically flailing and I was screaming, "Wait, what?!?! Are you fucking kidding me? You do realize I just walked in the door? Literally, two minutes ago. I walked in that door (I pointed). We were just laughing and making small talk a couple of minutes ago. Talking about previous tours and people we know in common. And then you put this on me? You give me this?! This is my first Consular tour. I don't know what the hell I'm doing yet! You can't give me this job! I'm not ready! I'm not prepared! Let someone else do it that has already acclimated to this fucking place!"

In actuality, I simply raised my eyebrows and muttered, "Oh…OK," before half walking, half stumbling into the cubicle I'd been told was my new office space for the year. I almost fell into my chair. Staring at the gray cubicle walls, but not seeing anything in particular, I steeled myself for what was to come. I sat, in dread, the enormity of the task washing over me. Not wanting to disappoint my boss on my first day and knowing I could not procrastinate much longer, I let out a deep breath and unwillingly flipped open the file and read its contents. Desperately wishing the entire time that I could click my heels together and magically get sent back home.

The deceased had been one of the many contractors in Iraq doing the logistics work necessary to keep our military up and running. He'd just happened to be on the wrong side of the road at the wrong time. I'd had a daylong or half-day long State Department training on how to perform death notifications. Seated hunched over, elbows on my desk, my hands intertwined in my hair, I stared down at the Department of Defense Medical Examiner's report in the folder, willing myself to focus and take in the contents of the report. I remembered that I was supposed to behave like an emotionless robot, keeping calm and collected, delivering the facts and not, definitely not, crying. Basically, what someone would expect from a stuffy, mindless bureaucrat.

Lifting my head up enough to look at my watch, I calculated the time difference and realized it was still early enough in the evening back home to call his wife. Taking another deep breath, I picked up the phone and dialed the home number. The deceased's adult daughter answered. I identified myself and my position and asked to speak to her mother. I can't recall if I was on speaker or if the daughter was simply relaying information to her mother who was standing nearby. I do remember that I immediately heard the mother and wife begin to cry when she found out who was on the phone. The daughter assured me any information for her mother could go through her. My job was made slightly easier by the fact that the family had already been notified by the contracting company that he was deceased, they just needed additional information on what would happen next. As I'd been instructed, I passed along the necessary information to the daughter about the current location of her father, the process for returning him to the United States, and when the family could expect to be reunited with him. At that point I thought the call was over. I did my job. I maintained composure. I was the perfect emotionless bureaucrat. Swiping away imaginary dirt from my keyboard with my fingertips, I began to breathe a little easier thinking the call hadn't been as gut-wrenchingly difficult as I had feared.

Then the daughter threw me for a loop—knocking me off my emotionless robot stand. She asked me to describe the damage done to her father. She said she wanted to know the condition of her father's body after he'd been blown up by a bomb.

Maintaining my composure as much as possible, I said something to the effect, "I believe that would best be discussed in person with your funeral home director."

She said, "I would like to know now."

And I said again, slightly more forcefully this time, "I think it would be better if you heard the details, in person, from your funeral home."

And she said, "No. I really want to know now."

Trying desperately to hide the fact that my stoic façade was beginning to crack, I tried to dissuade her for a third time, and stammered something like, "Are you sure? The extent and nature of his injuries may be distressing. I'm not sure that it's best for me to tell you over the phone."

She continued to insist, "I want to know—now."

White-knuckling the phone and not able to refuse her any longer, I simply said, "I have the Medical Examiner's Report in front of me. It's very clinical in nature. Do you want me to read it, or would you rather I summarize the contents," uncertain if I was following protocol or even allowed to say this. I was completely out on a limb. It was my first day on the job.

She said, "You can summarize."

Taking yet another deep breath, I stated, "Half his head is missing, his left elbow is mostly gone, and he's sustained damage to…" Honestly, I've blocked most of this part of the conversation out. But the daughter's next question was one I will never forget.

His daughter then asked, "But his hands are intact, right? His hands are OK?"

I wasn't sure why she was asking about her dad's hands. I frowned as I rescanned the ME report, and said, almost hesitantly, "From what I'm reading, it would appear that his hands are fine."

She replied, "Good. OK. Well, my mom says if his hands are intact, she can identify him then, by his hands. She'll know it's him by his hands."

At that point, my training went out the window, and we both started bawling. Not just a few tears slipping down my face, but openly, loudly sobbing. I'm not even sure how or when I finally hung up the phone. I was, however, a smoker at the time—and after that call—I grabbed my pack of cigarettes and lighter, and dodging my colleagues, I ran out of my cubicle, and blindly made my way to the front door. I hunched over and smoked a couple in a row, head in my hands, desperately trying to regain my composure, wondering what the hell I had gotten myself into. If I hadn't been on the front steps of the U.S. Embassy, I would have been curled up in a ball, rocking back and forth.

Calming down wasn't easy. Not only was the call replaying in my head in an endless heartbreaking loop, particularly the part about the wife identifying her dead husband by his intact hands, I could now hear a near constant barrage of gunfire coming from across the Tigris River. Unseen over the concrete barricade topped with curled razor wire, I knew insurgents were out there. To top it off, the air was heavy with the heat and dust of a late Baghdad summer. My surroundings were deafening and felt like they were closing in. "Maybe getting posted to the visa mill in Nigeria would have been a better bet," I thought to myself. "At least then I would have only had to reject visa applicants, who were trying to illegally overstay their time in America. And maybe deal with malaria or some other disease, but not this. Nothing like this! Nothing like talking to a daughter about her dead father, who was blown up by a bomb, first thing in the morning on day one on the job." It's difficult to remain detached and emotionless when someone's world is falling apart right in front of you. And I didn't want to ever get to the point where I became so numb that I could.

All of a sudden, serving one year in Baghdad didn't feel as "easy" as I had hoped.

CHAPTER 2:

Rewind

In what feels like a previous lifetime, I was a Foreign Service Officer with the U.S. Department of State. It was not a career I had planned for myself. In fact, I was well into adulthood before I realized it was a career. A daughter of farmers, I grew up in a large, Catholic family in a small lakeside town in Minnesota. Not all towns in Minnesota can be described as "lakeside," although a good many can given the state's 11,842 or so of them. My dad worked twelve hours a day in a lead factory that made fishing sinkers and car batteries. My mom stayed home with us six kids, making ends meet by clipping coupons and babysitting the neighborhood kids. Our family values consisted of hard work, common sense, and meaning what you said or only saying what you meant.

Every Sunday morning, after we got home from church and changed out of our Sunday best, it was my job to pick out a record to play for the family as we all gathered together in the living room. I had a particular fondness for "Flowers on the Wall" by the Statler Brothers and "Sink the Bismarck" by Johnny Horton. My Dad would fall into his "Dad Chair," a blue corduroy Lazy Boy, lean back, and put his feet up on the footrest. More often than not, there would be holes showing in the bottom of his black Sunday socks as he rubbed his feet together and read the *St. Paul Pioneer Press.* My older siblings fought over who got to read the comics first. Being the fifth of six siblings and the baby of the family for five years, I knew how to avoid the fray as much as possible. If I wasn't careful, I was liable to get a bruised shin or blackened eye by my brother who was two years my senior. My mom would sit on the 1980s floral fabric couch with the grocery store ads and scissors in hand, finding all the best deals and organizing them away in her wallet-sized coupon organizer.

Despite my parents raising six kids on the salary of a factory worker, I never wanted for anything. My parents made sure of that. They always put us kids first. My needs were met. And yet, I dreamed of more.

I would often think that I was destined for something bigger than my little lakeside town and that my life had a purpose beyond myself, if that makes sense. Every time I had that thought though, I would immediately be washed in shame and guilt—feeling narcissistic for having thoughts of grandeur or for being too big for my britches or for wanting too much. Looking back at my childhood, I'm not sure where that feeling came from, why I felt guilty or self-absorbed for being ambitious. It feels cliché and easy to say so, but maybe Catholic guilt really is learned early, if that's what it was. Regardless, I stayed cocooned in my small community.

Until the summer before fifth grade, in the mid-1980s, the world came to me. For some reason, my parents decided to host an exchange student from Germany for a month. I openly stared at her hairy legs and armpits. I was already old enough to be aware that women and even teenage girls were supposed to shave their legs and armpits. I questioned her sanity when she rode her bike down the middle of the highway, *like she was in a car.* I was shocked by her unfamiliarity with peanut butter. "Who doesn't know about peanut butter," I asked myself. And I wrinkled my nose at the strange smelling floral body lotion she liberally used instead of showering. My sister recently reminded me that I never showered regularly as a kid, mostly I bathed twice a week, whether I needed it or not. However, even by my low standards, the exchange student apparently didn't shower enough. My parents actually had to sit her down and talk to her about hygiene. I imagine that must have been pretty awkward for all of them.

Regardless of her eccentricities, at least to a ten-year-old, she opened my eyes to the idea that there really was a bigger world out there, beyond my small town. I became curious about life in other countries, about people from other places. And, decided that I wanted to travel and learn about not only what makes us different but also what makes us the same.

I got my first chance to travel internationally in high school (well other than making various quick trips to Canada, which is pretty common for Minnesotans, and doesn't feel so international). My German teacher told me about the Congress-Bundestag Youth Exchange (CBYE) program, a joint US–German Government scholarship for exchange students. Each year, hundreds of American high school students are placed in German homes and hundreds of German kids are sent all over the United States under CBYE. The program started in 1983 to commemorate the 300th anniversary of Germans settling in North America.

I anxiously filled out the application for the program and trepidatiously traveled to "The Cities" (i.e., somewhere around St. Paul or Minneapolis) for an oral interview. When I received the notification in the mail a few weeks later that I'd been chosen to be one of the scholarship recipients, I uncharacteristically jumped around whooping (just one whoop though, I didn't want to get too carried away). It would be an understatement to say that my family was not very emotionally expressive. My husband jokes that using the same tone of voice, my mother would deliver the news that they'd won the lottery and that Uncle Bob had died (not that I have an Uncle Bob). But you get the point—growing up, our emotional scale ranged from about a 4.5 to a 5.5. Putting all that into context, jumping and one whoop was a big deal—I was excited!

And then, a few months later, off I went to spend my high school senior year abroad. I absolutely fell in love with traveling and language and new ideas and my German host family. They took me right in and immediately made me a part of their family. Most Sundays, my two host siblings and me would pile into my host parents' room and all have breakfast in bed together. To this day, I'm still in contact my host parents, Mama and Papa.

In college, I spent my sophomore year studying in Akita, Japan. The Minnesota State University system had an extension college in Akita, so I was able to study in Japan for the same in state tuition rate I was accustomed to. I found it a more challenging culture to adapt to than that in Germany, as my proclivity for independence and outspokenness was not always well-received in a country that has an oft-repeated saying, "The nail that stands up, gets hammered down." And yet, I found my people. A handful of Japanese students took me in and made me part of their close-knit community.

In graduate school, I interned in Geneva, Switzerland at the International Organization for Migration (IOM). At the time, the IOM was involved in processing claims for World War II non-Jewish concentration camp victims. I was chosen by the IOM because between undergraduate and graduate school, I worked for over two years processing claims as part of a multistate class action lawsuit against Prudential Insurance. Obviously vastly different circumstances, but the behind-the-scenes mechanics of processing claims was surprisingly similar.

After all this travel, it was no shock to my family when I announced that I was majoring in International Relations and that, specifically, I wanted to become an international negotiator. Ever the ambitious optimist, I envisioned myself at some big important peace table, helping countries find win–

win solutions, bridging gaps, and building peace. But alas, at twenty-five, I did not follow that path. I located only one private firm that specialized in providing international negotiators without law degrees, and they were not hiring. So instead, a graduate school friend told me I should sign up to take the State Department's Foreign Service Exam with him. "It's another option," he said. To which I responded without really knowing the details, "Why not. I don't have anything else going on." I like making major life decisions rashly.

CHAPTER 3:

The Foreign Service

I am one of those lucky (some people might call it nerdy) people who love tests. I love them. I like filling in the bubbles. I like being the first one done. And I enjoy the pressure of writing essays under a deadline; it gives me a rush. Plus, I usually excel at test taking (I never claimed to be modest). So, I followed my friend's advice, took the Foreign Service written and oral exams, and passed. My memories of the daylong oral exam will forever be clouded by another woman who also took hers that same day.

As instructed via a letter, in the fall of 2001, I walked into a nondescript office building in Washington DC, rode the elevator to the assigned floor at the appointed time, and found my way to a waiting room. As I nervously glanced around, anxious for what was to come, I thought my surroundings were disappointingly similar to the countless waiting rooms I'd sat in before: the same industrial carpeting, the same soothing colored walls, the same generic artwork, and the same molded chairs with cushioned seats lining the edges of the room. There was a watercooler in one corner and a plant in the other. I'm not sure what I was expecting, but it felt altogether anticlimactic for a day that could literally change the course of my life.

After a few minutes of nervously glancing about and furtively checking out the other applicants who arrived before me, another woman came in and slid into the seat next to me. She flashed me an anxious smile. We appeared to be the only two women out of the dozen or so people who were there that day for the oral exam, so it felt natural to sit next to each other. My first thought was, "Yay, another woman, maybe we can keep each other company and support one another throughout the day." Turning to face me, she introduced herself and said she was a student at Johns Hopkins School of Advanced International Studies. I responded, letting her know I was a student at the Maxwell School at Syracuse University. Almost before the word "University" was out of my mouth, with a look of derision and a saccharine tone, she said, "At my school, at SAIS, I attended a prep session with a former Ambassador. And he said we should really only wear a blue or black pants suit on the day of the oral examination if we wanted to pass." I didn't need to glance down at myself to know I was wearing a tan skirt suit.

My eyebrows furrowing, I stared at her for a minute, and thought, "What is wrong with you? We're the only women here. We're supposed to be allies; we should be supporting each other and celebrating our success. Why are you trying to psych me out right before the exam? Not cool. Not cool at all, dude."

I gathered my runaway thoughts and returned the lob in the most unconcerned voice I could muster, "Well, at my school, at Maxwell, I also attended a prep session with a former Ambassador. And he said we should wear whatever makes us feel the most comfortable and confident." (A belated thank you to Ambassador Levitsky for his advice).

While not my proudest moment, I have to admit there was some satisfaction in knowing that I passed the exam that day and she did not. Those of us who passed were asked to stay behind to immediately start the security clearance interview process, those who didn't pass had to parade by us as they walked out the waiting room door. As she passed me, head hanging, she looked up for a brief moment and muttered under her breath, "Congrats." In reply, I beamed, "Thanks!" just managing to contain myself from doing a victory fist pump or a cartwheel, tan skirt suit be damned.

After exam day and the required security clearance background check were completed, I was called up for service into a new class of Foreign Service Officers that started in November 2002. I didn't know what to expect. I was simply filled with the buoyant optimism of a privileged twenty-something who was figuring out what door to open next.

Foreign Service Officers are employees of the U.S. Department of State. State Department employees also include Foreign Service Specialists, Civil Servants (primarily based at DC headquarters), locally employed staff at embassies and consulates, and various classes of political appointees. All combined, the State Department represents the interests of the United States in foreign countries. They staff the roughly 300 U.S. embassies, consulates, and diplomatic missions around the world, as well as the State Department headquarters in Washington, DC.

There are five Foreign Service Officer specializations called "cones": Political, Economic, Public Affairs, Management, and Consular. I was an Economics Officer (of course I was, the Economics Officers are usually the nerdiest ones). As much as I hate admitting it, my high school guidance counselor was right. I was meant to work with numbers. He had encouraged me to major in math in college, as it was my strong suit, but ever the nerdy rebel, I, I thought math was "too easy." I wanted to travel the world and opted for Political Science and International Relations instead. And yet, ultimately, as an Econ-coned officer, there I was pouring over numbers and data and graphs and statistics. I once told a visiting roomful of high-profile and well-educated guests in Dubai that "numbers are important" to Economic Officers. That self-evident statement got a bit of a laugh—at me.

Like with any organization, there is an unstated, yet ever-present hierarchy, among the various types of officers. My information is slightly dated now, and other Foreign Service Officers may disagree about the order of this hierarchy, but Political Officers are definitely the cool kids at any embassy. When I took the Foreign Service Exam, a higher score was necessary to become a political officer, presumably because it was much more popular than the other cones. Political Officers are charged with understanding the political environment of the country where they are posted and reporting that information back to Washington. They have meetings with all the big, important political muckety-mucks.

The not-quite-as-cool younger sibling of the Political Officer is the Economic Officer, who is tasked with determining the economic situation on the ground. I once had a boss (also an Economic Officer) who told me partly in jest that Political Officers may think they're the best—but they often find themselves having coffee with political dissidents who can barely rub two cents together; while Economic Officers go to dinner at the best restaurants in town with CEOs and other business leaders. I'm not sure if he really believed that (possibly) or if it was just a pep talk for my chosen path (more likely), which had rendered me perpetually in second place in the embassy hierarchy. I try not to show it, but I can be obnoxiously competitive, as can my husband. Our kids are going to need *so* much therapy. We half-jokingly say that in our family, second place is the first loser (with great emphasis on *loser*).

Public Affairs Officers (PAOs) generally come third, although some may think they are on the same level as Economic Officers. PAOs fill two main functions: speaking to the press and overseeing cultural programs or exchanges. Originally, I thought about being a Public Affairs Officer, with my positive student exchange experiences in high school and college, but the idea of talking to the press scared me. Still does. I feel compelled to forthrightly answer every question asked of me, which is probably an unfortunate trait for those tasked with speaking with the press, particularly government officials who deal in classified materials. Once while in Dubai, my boss sent me to talk about Iran's economy with a well-known journalist named Robin Wright. I was so petrified of accidently leaking classified information or saying something wrong thing that I'm sure I came across as a tongue-tied bumbling idiot not worthy of her time.

Next are the Management Officers. They are in charge of everything that keeps an embassy running, as well as moving and housing of Foreign Service personnel. Think motor pool, arranging airfare, apartment leases, maintenance of embassy grounds, and so on. While management jobs are not as cool as some of the other overseas postings, Management Officers often have the last laugh. Because they showcase their management skills early on, by being in charge of large budgets and the most personnel, they can also set themselves up for assignments that require strong management skills like ambassadorships.

Consular Officers, the fifth and final cone, perform two main functions: visa interviews for both immigrant and non-immigrant travelers to the United States and American Citizen Services (ACS). Conducting visa interviews is a painful and thankless job. Consular employees are at the front lines in deciding which foreigners can or cannot present themselves at a United States border, but they are often under pressure to complete interviews quickly while dealing with yelling, crying, lying, and all sorts of other human behavior—good and bad. Their snap decisions can literally change a person's life. It's a lot of pressure.

ACS assists Americans who are traveling overseas with all matters of life, such as birth, death, illness, incarceration, lost passports, notarizing documents, and more. ACS can also be an unappreciated job. During office hours, ACS is the responsibility of the Consular Officers, but on nights and weekends, American embassy or consulate staff rotate being the off-hours

ACS "duty officer" for a week at a time. There is a designated "duty phone" and log book that is passed around. Whenever it was my turn, I would plead to the Consular Gods for a quiet week. It didn't always work. One time I was woken up in the middle of the night because an American citizen, and college student, had been taken into custody at the Dubai Airport and needed help. He had trace amounts of marijuana in his wallet. Dubai has a zero-tolerance policy for drugs. Possession, or in this case, evidence of previous possession is punishable by years in prison. I took down his information and the information about where he was being held to pass to the Consular Officers. It would be their job to visit the American in jail and make sure he was receiving proper treatment and due process under the local law. Contrary to what some Americans may believe, if an American commits a crime overseas, as defined by the laws of the country they are in, the U.S. Government cannot get them out of jail. It can only make sure that the American is being properly cared for and legally represented. Depending on the nature and circumstances of the situation, it may advocate for release or for a lesser punishment, but the U.S. Government has to respect local laws.

The Consular Section of any given embassy or consulate usually requires the most bodies, so regardless of a Foreign Service Officer's specialty or cone, everyone is required to serve as a Consular Officer for at least one year during their first or second overseas posting or tour. I filled an Economic Officer job for my first tour, so I reluctantly had to work as a Consular Officer for my second. I cannot overstate how much I dreaded the thought of processing visas, which to me exemplified bureaucratic drudgery (no offense to Consular Officers).

A State Department "tour" typically lasts one to three years, depending on if the post is considered dangerous and the officer's level of seniority. Occasionally, officers have the opportunity to extend their tours, but it is not always guaranteed. Every one to three years or so, Foreign Service Officers begin a new job, in a new foreign location, with new coworkers and responsibilities and are immediately expected to become highly functioning experts in their field—and answer the most nuanced questions required of their position for bosses, Congressional delegations, the press, and the American public. The move could be to a neighboring country—or across the world to a totally new continent.

Over the course of six years, I worked in five U.S. embassies and consulates across the Middle East and North Africa: Tunisia, Libya, Bahrain, Iraq, and the United Arab Emirates. The constant moving and acclimating to new and different jobs was not as difficult as it may sound, Foreign Service Officers always have tremendous support. Depending on the size of the mission, hundreds or even thousands of local employees staff embassies overseas; while civil servants staff the headquarters in Washington. These staff provide a level of consistency and institutional knowledge necessary to keep things running, despite the high officer turnover rates (overseas tours are deliberately kept short to prevent Americans from "going native" or becoming apologists for their host nation).

The local staff, who are primarily residents of the embassy or consulate host country, are outstanding employees who go above and beyond their job requirements, making life easier for the American officers. Sometimes, they can be almost too conscientious. One time, a local employee in Libya went *way* beyond his duties, resulting in a very embarrassing professional moment for me.

It was the spring of 2004. Colonel Qadhafi (former Libyan military official who, in 1969, staged a coup and overthrew King Idris to become Libya's head of state. He was known for penning *The Green Book*, his proclivity for female security guards and his rambling hours-long television addresses) decided to surrender his weapons of mass destruction—triggering talks to resume relations with the United States. U.S. relations soured after Reagan sanctioned air strikes against Libya in 1986 in retaliation for a Berlin terrorist bombing. Not to mention when the Libyans shot down Pan Am Flight 103 over Lockerbie, Scotland in 1988, killing all 259 people onboard, including

189 Americans and 11 residents of Lockerbie whose neighborhood was hit by the burning plane.

Prior to the United States lifting sanctions in 2004, which had been in place for nearly twenty years, a handful of State Department employees were temporarily sent to Tripoli to begin the process of resuming diplomatic ties. I was in neighboring Tunisia working as an Economic/Commercial Officer and, to be honest, my plate was not full. Not much was happening in Tunisia at the time. I was doing lots of fun stuff, like escorting American astronauts who were visiting on goodwill missions around town, but nothing that would be considered timely or urgent. As a result, Washington decided that I'd be a good choice to send to Tripoli for three months to figure out how Americans could do business in Libya. Because of the sanctions, the United States had been barred from the Libyan oil fields for nearly two decades, and U.S. oil companies had itchy feet, particularly since five years earlier, European companies had been allowed back in when the United Nations lifted its sanctions. My job was to draft the first, post-sanctions Country Commercial Guide, a U.S. Department of Commerce document that provides support to American entities wishing to do business abroad. It covers everything from setting up phone lines, to regulations around property ownership and local representation.

Some of my business contacts in Tunisia had connections to folks in Tripoli—so I was able to start the ball rolling and set up a couple of meetings with Libyans before I even left town.

I was not the first State Department employee to arrive in Tripoli; a couple of others had already arrived before me. They were kind enough to send a local to the airport to meet me and take me to the Corinthia Hotel in Tripoli, which would be my home for three months. The nice, young Libyan man who met me in the arrival hall, whom I shall call Ahmed, was no doubt spying on us for the Libyan Government, as we were the first American Government employees in town in a long time. Ahmed was our go-to person for everything: translator, chauffeur, cultural interpreter, airport expediter, and errand runner. One of his frequent duties was taking our laundry to a local laundromat, so we didn't have to pay the exorbitant hotel laundry prices.

Several weeks after my arrival, I donned my fanciest suit and pearls (pearls are the ultimate in diplomat fashion). And I pulled my hair back into a harsh bun at the nape of my neck, for a meeting with an old-school Libyan Government official in the Oil & Gas Sector. Still in my twenties, but consciously aware that I looked like a teenager, I did my best to dress the part of a diplomat to counter my youthful appearance.

We were deep into a talk on foreign oil company operations in Libya, when my cell phone began ringing. I discretely looked down at the screen and saw that it was Ahmed. Silencing the call and ignoring the interruption, I continued with what I was saying. Then he called again. I silenced and ignored the call a second time, slightly annoyed by his willful interruption of my meeting. Ahmed knew where I was, he had dropped me off at the Ministry. But when he called for the third time, in a matter of seconds—I decided I'd better answer, he was sending the universally recognized signal that it was something important. I had no idea what was going on. Apologizing to the Libyan official, I turned my head slightly away and accepted the call. Ahmed was one of those loud talkers. The kind where I could hold the phone a foot away from my ear and still hear what he was saying, and so could the Libyan.

Launching right in, broadcasting loud enough for the Libyan official to hear, Ahmed said, "Amy, I am at the laundromat, and you wrote down that you were turning in six pair of panties, but I only count five."

Flushing, my tongue practically tripped over itself as I rushed to get out the words, "Five is fine, just go with five."

Ignoring my response completely, he continued, "Now that I have you on the phone, let me count one more time, one…two…three…four…five… yes, five, I definitely only count five." Frozen, and subconsciously squeezing my eyes shut, I silently hoped he wouldn't go on to say, "Here's the black pair, the red pair…"

Burying my head as deeply as possible into my right hand, hoping to cover my blushing cheeks and muffle my mortified voice, I said, "It's fine. Just forget the sixth. It's OK. Five is fine."

Obstinately oblivious to anything but his accurately carrying out his job, he continued, "Are you sure? I can check through all your laundry one more time. Maybe the sixth pair is stuck to another piece of your clothing."

Terrified of what would happen if the conversation were allowed to continue, I said, "I'm sure. Five is fine. Thank you. Goodbye." I'm sure my "goodbye" was cut off midway in my rush to hang up.

As I got off the phone and reluctantly turned my head back around, I caught the eye of the Libyan official. Although his face gave nothing away, I could tell he'd heard the entire exchange. But with the diplomatic tact, which is expected of our stations, we got right back to business.

In addition to the strides we made that day for the future of U.S. oil companies in Libya, I firmly believe that somewhere in the annals of the Libyan Ministry of Oil files, there are notes about the number of panties I had laundered. Either that or some Libyan guy still has my sixth pair—I think it might have been the red ones.

CHAPTER 4:

I Have to Go Where?

My three months in Libya could fill an entire book by itself. I had so many singular experiences. Like when I was leaving the country for good to return to Tunisia and was told at the airport that I couldn't leave without an "exit visa." When the Libyan Border Patrol Officer said I needed an exit visa to get on the plane, I gaped at him like I didn't understand English, repeating in a slow and stilted voice, "Ex-it Vi-sa?"

"Yes, exit visa," he assertively confirmed. I wasn't sure what the hell was going on. No one on the Tunisian Embassy staff had mentioned this possibility when they made my travel arrangements. Countries typically require visas for foreigners to enter, not to exit their borders, particularly diplomats who usually fall under some special status agreement. Realizing I wasn't going to change the border guard's mind on my own, I had no choice but to turn around and return to the Corinthia Hotel. On the drive back with Ahmed, staring absent-mindedly out the window, I speculated the various reasons that I wasn't being allowed to leave. Perhaps the Libyans had lost face in their negotiations with the United States that week and this was how they were showing their power and control over America. In the end, I gave up and just assumed that someone, somewhere in the Libyan Government was messing with me for no good reason beyond—they could.

I called and let my colleagues in Tripoli know what had happened and I said that I needed my room at the hotel again. I'll never forget walking back through the front doors of the Corinthia, and one of my coworkers serenading me with *Hotel California* by the Eagles. He seemed to think he was particularly amusing as he sang, *"Welcome to the Hotel Corinthia, such a lovely place, such a lovely face…you can check out any time you like, but you can never leave."* "Yeah, very funny," I said sarcastically.

Appealing to those above my pay grade for assistance, a couple of calls to Libya's Ministry of Foreign Affairs, and a few days later, I was inexplicably finally allowed to leave, but a sticker was added to my passport indicating that I could never return. I was PNGed from Libya (declared Persona Non Grata, meaning I was not allowed to return—although this may no longer be the case given the change in government there). The strange thing was that there was no explanation by the Libyan Government why I was PNGed or at least not to me. In my experience, it's pretty rare for a diplomat to be PNGed, I don't know of anyone else that ever was (except my sister when she was working for Habitat for Humanity International in Russia. But that was a whole different thing, and it was Russia, and she wasn't a government employee). Regardless of the reason, I was fine to go. I completed the task and drafted the first U.S. Country Commercial Guide for Libya in nearly twenty years. I returned to my actual assignment in Tunisia. For as sleepy of a post as it was at the time, I still had a job to do there.

Back in Tunis, I continued with my economics job. I'd been in the job for a year and felt more confident. I built good working relations with my Tunisian counterparts and created some great contacts with business leaders, all of which helped in my reports back to DC. Then, the State Department Washington decision makers decided to pull me away from Tunisia a second time and sent me to Bahrain for six months. Apparently, I'd done a good enough job on my first temporary assignment, that I was shifted around yet again when a junior officer left Manama and the Department had a gap to fill in Bahrain. The United States had just signed a Free Trade Agreement with Bahrain, and the Economic Officer had to return home for personal reasons. It was unusual to serve in three countries during one tour, and my Deputy Chief of Mission (DCM) in Tunisia (number two at an embassy behind the Ambassador) wasn't happy. I think he blamed me for repeatedly losing a body at his post (he even tried to bad mouth me on my employee review, which I fought with the help of my new boss in Bahrain). What the DCM seemed to willfully misunderstand was that as a first tour officer, I didn't really have a choice. A Foreign Service Officer's first two tours are "directed." This means that while officers submit a list of their preferred postings to the HR department (from available jobs), HR ultimately decides where Entry Level Officers go. What I didn't tell my DCM in Tunisia was that had I been given a choice; I enthusiastically would have agreed to go to Bahrain. I was being given the chance to have all sorts of exciting adventures beyond the scope of a typical first tour.

Shortly before departing for my six-month temporary assignment in Bahrain, I was informed that for my second tour, I would be going to Baghdad, Iraq for one year to complete my Consular requirement, starting late summer 2005. As mentioned, Consular Officers perform visa work (immigrant and nonimmigrant interviews) and provide American Citizen Services (helping Americans overseas with all matters of life).

Baghdad was a mess at the time. The second Gulf War had just been fought in 2003. The news coming out of Iraq left me nervous and unsettled, and I usually don't get nervous. After all, I had just spent three months in Tripoli. Qadhafi was known to be unpredictable, so we never knew what the next day would bring in Libya. However, since my first tour was technically in the safe and lovely country of Tunisia (even though I was sent off to other, not as safe places), I drew the short straw and had to fulfill my consular tour in Baghdad. To be perfectly honest, I had a choice between one year in Baghdad or a two-year posting at a visa mill in Nigeria.

A "visa mill" refers to embassies or consulates with high numbers of visa applicants. Think Mexico City and the Philippines and Nigeria. Consular Officers in high-traffic visa mills can often literally interview hundreds of applicants a day. There are dedicated, lifelong Consular Officers who choose this work, but for most Foreign Service Officers, they put in the minimum amount of Consular work required. And standing on my feet at a visa window in Nigeria, the days endlessly stringing together as I interviewed countless visa applicants, seemed like a horrible way to spend two years.

I was not looking forward to the boring, bureaucratic atmosphere of a consular tour, but I especially loathed the idea of serving at a visa mill in Nigeria, so I put Baghdad higher on my preference list—as I thought, "Hey, how bad can one year in Baghdad be? I can do anything for one year."

Side Note: The first two Junior Officer tours are typically two years long each. Because Baghdad was considered dangerous, the tour there was only one year, whereas a consular tour in Nigeria would have been two years.

Once Foreign Service Officers are promoted to mid-level officers (typically by or in their third tour), they have more say in where they end up. Then the "bidding process" requires lobbying for each of their successive postings, networking, and using their connections to try and secure their top choice. I didn't stick around long enough to really see this in action, but apparently the higher up officers get, the more brutal the bidding process becomes. There's reportedly drama and backstabbing and all sorts of shenanigans as people compete over the most desirable postings. And sometimes it's completely out of the officer's control. When I was first assigned to Tunisia, but still in Washington, a few other officers who were also going to Tunis and I had dinner with our presumptive Ambassador. He was a longtime Middle East expert, well-liked, and well-respected in the State Department. His Senate confirmation to the position (the Senate confirms all Ambassadorial appointments) seemed like a shoo-in. However, at his Senate confirmation hearing, according to the State Department rumor mill, it reportedly came out that while he was serving in Jerusalem, a local newspaper attributed a pro-Palestinian remark to "a senior U.S. Government official." Although the source was not named and no one thought it was the presumed Ambassador to Tunisia, because he was the most senior U.S. Government official in Jerusalem at the time—the Senate held him responsible and did not confirm his Ambassadorship. The Ambassadorship was supposed to be his reward after many long years of service to the United States in hardship postings across the Middle East, and just like that, it was gone because of an errant statement that was likely made by one of his employees or a visiting official.

Due to my series of temporary duty assignments, Baghdad would be my second tour as a Foreign Service Officer—but Iraq was actually the fourth Middle Eastern country I'd worked in for the State Department, after Tunisia, Libya, and Bahrain.

CHAPTER 5:

War Zone Training

Between Bahrain and Baghdad, I was sent back to Washington DC to attend Consular Officer Training and a weeklong war zone preparedness class. Holing up in a boutique Kimpton hotel at the corner of O and 16th (which met government per diem rates), I was looking forward to my two months stateside before returning overseas. It was a chance to connect with other Foreign Service Officers who had also started in November 2002, eat at my favorite restaurants in town, and engage in some of my preferred DC summer activities, like renting a kayak from Key Bridge Boathouse and spending a couple of hours on the Potomac.

Before reporting for duty in Baghdad, I had to attend the requisite two-month course on how to adjudicate visas and provide American Citizen Services. The training was held at the Foreign Service Institute (FSI) in Arlington, Virginia. It's the State Department's educational campus, where it prepares employees to perform the various required job duties, as well as teach foreign languages when needed. A lot of the Consular class focused on visa types and classifications and legal mumbo jumbo—pretty boring stuff. My favorite class was the day we learned about micro-expressions. Using a computer game and watching television coverage of convicted criminals initially denying their crimes, we had to intently watch people's facial expressions for the .4- to .5-second flash of emotions such as amusement, embarrassment, anxiety, guilt, pride, relief, contentment, pleasure, or shame and correctly identify it. When people show contempt, guilt, or shame, they are probably lying about something. Or at the very least, there's something they're hiding. The bottom line in the context of Consular Officer work, no visa to the United States for them.

I still apply micro-expression recognition in my life today, carefully watching faces for that emotional split-second reaction. Much to the chagrin of my husband, if I think he's upset, I'll climb onto his lap and get up in his face and read any micro-expressions he might reveal.

I also underwent five days of war zone preparedness training. I spent one day learning how to shoot four different types of guns. I think there was a rifle, a pistol of some sort, an A-something, and a B-something. This might sound flippant, but I'd never held a gun before and didn't really have the desire to. I'm a hippie at heart—I feel like I was born thirty years too late. My favorite music is 1960s rock, like *Stop Children What's That Sound* by Buffalo Springfield. In college, I wore bell-bottoms and flowing, flowered shirts.

Despite my protestations about handling firearms, the ex-military instructor who taught us how to break down the guns, put them back together, and shoot them, said to me, rather firmly, "This training is necessary in case the military convoy escorting you around Iraq is incapacitated—you'll need to pick up one of their weapons and know how to defend yourself." I left class thinking if I had to pick up a gun again, I'd probably only know enough to accidentally shoot myself in the foot—seriously. I wasn't really sure if the few hours of training had been helpful for someone like me who had zero gun skills to begin with and no desire to change that. Luckily my gun knowledge, or lack thereof, was never tested (spoiler alert).

During my weapons training, a local Washington DC news affiliate happened to be doing a short piece on diplomats preparing to go into a war zone. I was the only woman in class that day—so naturally they focused on me. They must have thought it would make a better story, "Nerdy, pacifist, female diplomat gets gun training to go to Baghdad." Or maybe I just looked good in my multipocketed cargo pants and solid T-shirt, the de rigueur for civilians heading to Baghdad.

The news team edited this awesome clip of me shooting and hitting the target, but it was actually another classmate who hit the bull's eye. That was really very nice of them as I came across like a skilled shot. I never had the opportunity to thank the editors. While writing this, I combed through archives trying find the old news footage—but no luck. It must have been in July or August 2005. (If any enterprising readers locate it, please send me a copy. I'm pretty confident it was the Washington DC ABC affiliate.)

We also spent a day doing spy training stuff, like learning how to spot a surveillance detection team while driving. It was interesting but I wasn't very good at it, mostly I just guessed, it felt like one big game to me. It was difficult to take seriously as it seemed so far removed from my economic analysis desk job and meeting government officials. I tried not to show my lack of seriousness. It was, after all, much more fun driving around Virginia trying to figure out what cars were tailing us rather than sitting in class learning about different visa classifications. I was pretty giddy and smiling ear to ear, as I asked our instructors with unrestrained excitement, "Ohh…is it the red jeep that's following us? Did I get it? Did I get it? Am I right? Or (turning and pointing out the passenger side window) maybe it's that tan sedan?"

I really wanted to take the aggressive driving course diplomats that had gone to Baghdad before me got to do. I'd heard that in addition to defensive driving, they learned super-fun maneuvers like turning out of a skid and peel-outs, and using the hand brake to flip around. But I was told it was no longer necessary. The instructors said, "now independent movement for State Department employees is restricted to Baghdad's Green Zone" and I wouldn't be doing any driving. My instructors lied. I did drive in the Green Zone a.k.a. the International Zone (IZ)—every day. It's a good thing I never went above twenty-five miles per hour; otherwise, that aggressive driving class might have come in handy, if I had to make a fast getaway. Not that anyone drove fast in the Green Zone, there were too many internal checkpoints scattered throughout for that.

A photo of me with my car in Baghdad's Green Zone in the Fall of 2005. This was taken near my office, so you can see the concrete barriers and razor wire that separated the road from the Tigris River (as mentioned in Chapter 1).

Close to the end of my war zone preparedness class, an American woman who'd survived the 2003 bombing of the Al-Rashid Hotel in Baghdad spoke to us about her experience. On October 26, 2003, an American colonel was killed and at least sixteen people were injured, when eight to ten missiles were launched from a homemade launchpad at the hotel (the exact number of missiles is unknown). It just so happened that Deputy Defense Secretary Paul Wolfowitz was staying at the hotel that night. He was Secretary of Defense and Donald Rumsfeld's number two, and although he's claimed otherwise, he is widely thought to be the architect of the Iraq War. The woman, a State Department employee, said she'd been peacefully sitting in her hotel room when the bombs hit. One of the explosions resulted in her arm nearly being torn off. Dazed, confused, and in shock, she stumbled down multiple flights of stairs and out the front of the hotel. All the while she fought off multiple military guys who wanted to put her arm in a tourniquet using their belts. She didn't want a tourniquet. She wanted to save her arm. She recounted how in her confused state she recalled some first-aid training about tourniquets and just knew she didn't want one because in all likelihood it would mean her arm would have to be amputated. The more she described the bombing and her harrowing escape from the collapsing building and the chaos, the more dread washed over me. I started feeling physically ill. Sitting there, I wondered if I could demonstrate a similar level of courage and awareness in the same situation. I wasn't sure since I'd never been tested in that way before. I was upset with myself for not taking the course more seriously. One week of playing spy, learning to shoot, and hearing about the realities of war did not feel like enough—it felt inadequate.

That whole week of war zone preparedness training, reminded me of my graduate school days. My International Relations concentration had been international negotiation and intercultural communication. I took a lot of courses on conflict resolution, negotiation, and peace building. One course had been a study of various United Nations peacekeeping missions. We'd discussed the long, complicated transitions militaries had to go through to get from being war makers to also being peacekeepers. It's a completely different skill set. We learned that the skills and training required to teach soldiers to maintain peace and security are quite different from those needed to hype them up to go on raids and shoot people.

Conversely, I felt like my war zone training was not nearly enough to ready a diplomat, a peacekeeper if you will, to an individual prepared for the rigors of a war zone. It wasn't what I had signed up for when I joined the State Department. I'd wanted to change the world with the use of words and building relationships, not by accidently shooting myself if my convoy was incapacitated by Iraqi insurgents. And not by losing a limb, as our guest speaker very nearly had. But I was being directed by the State Department to go to a war zone. It was either that or quit a job I really loved. And I didn't want to quit. The ten-year-old girl in me, from a small lakeside town in Minnesota, was proud that I was doing something to make a difference for our country.

Still, the closer my departure date, the more nervous I became. In any other situation, in any other country (perhaps with the exception of Afghanistan), diplomats would not have been allowed to serve in a country (like Iraq) with such a high level of danger present and where we were still fighting insurgents. Missiles were still being launched into the Green Zone. Under normal circumstances, most Foreign Service personnel would have all been long evacuated. But the political realities dictated I go. How would it look to the rest of the world if the United States couldn't send its people into a country where we had "won the war?"

On the final war zone training day, we were told to make plans—write goodbye letters, draw up a will, set up code words or signals with family in case we were kidnapped and videotaped so we could send a secret or hidden message. I never talked to my family about it. While perhaps practical, it just felt too surreal, too macabre. Plus, I figured my parents were already worried enough. But it was on that rather dark note that I said goodbye to my family and friends and left for Iraq the following week.

CHAPTER 6:

Getting to Baghdad

Getting to Baghdad, Iraq in 2005 was not a simple proposition. The first stop was at a military base in the DC area to get a CAC card (a Common Access Card). Even though the Defense Department, via the Coalition Provisional Authority, had handed control of Iraq back to the Iraqis in June 2004—thereby turning control of U.S. Government interests over to the State Department—the military continued to be responsible for the logistics and comings and goings of Americans. Put simply, in times of war, the military is in command; in times of peace, the State Department is in charge—but during modern conflicts, there can be a protracted period where departmental oversight overlaps. Needless to say, in 2005, to get in and out of Baghdad on military transport, I needed a Military ID.

Side note: As I just mentioned, after the second Gulf War, and before June 28, 2004—the U.S. Military oversaw U.S. interests in Baghdad. I wasn't there at the time of the transition, so don't quote me on this—but stories circulated that when the Defense Department transferred control of the Republican Palace to the State Department (Saddam's former palace in Baghdad housed most U.S. Government personnel offices)—the military took the fancy, secure doors from the palace with them (not sure if it was the front doors, or internal doors that protected classified materials). Talk about bureaucracy. The State Department had to find new doors. I'm sure Defense had their reasons. But the weeds do feel pretty cloying at times. After all, we all work(ed) for the same government.

Military ID in hand, I was ready for my commercial flights from Washington DC to Amman, Jordan's Marka Airport, via Frankfurt, Germany. I made it to Amman at 10 p.m. on September 3, 2005 and overnighted at the Amman Marriott Hotel before leaving for Baghdad the following morning. I ate my last meal, breakfast, before my flight to Baghdad. Scooting my chair in, I sat at an immaculately dressed dining table by myself, numbly chewing on a croissant and drinking a steaming cup of coffee in a white china cup way too small to give me the caffeine necessary to fortify myself for what was to come. I was so deep in thought, anxious about the day ahead, I don't remember if there were other guests milling about. I felt completely alone, and I didn't come across any other Americans on their way to Baghdad. Not to sound biblical, but it felt like a last supper or last breakfast before my flight to Iraq.

I felt condemned, unsure of what I'd find. I wasn't the first diplomat to travel to Baghdad post-second Gulf War, many had gone before me…other civilians had navigated in and out of the war zone just fine. But I was still nervous—super nervous. I was by myself, about to travel into a war zone with one week of training. One week. I knew I wasn't expected to go to the frontlines like some of our military, armed with weapons, directly confronting insurgents, but still. It would have been nice to travel with a team or at least one other person—someone to help calm my nerves and talk through the unknowns.

Finishing up my morning meal, I wiped my mouth, threw down the white cloth napkin on the table, and quickly returned to my room where I grabbed my backpack. In addition to the one backpack I was allowed to carry with me, I was allotted a 250-pound air shipment of clothes, toiletries, and nonperishable food items that was likely still in Washington DC waiting to be sent to Iraq on the next available cargo plane. I tried not to let my nerves show as I made my way back down the elevator to the lobby and checked out of the hotel. It was time to go. One of the staff from the U.S. Embassy in Jordan had arranged a car to take me from the hotel to the Queen Alia Airport where I had to find the U.S. Military transport C-130 plane that was going to fly me to Baghdad. I walked out the front doors of the Marriot and scanned the porte-cochere for my ride, ignoring the bustling traffic and noise of the street. I smiled unconsciously as I quickly and triumphantly spotted my driver. The Petra Tours vehicle was clearly marked and stood out among the other cars, much like I probably did, a twenty-nine-year-old American woman (who still looked like an undergraduate). I climbed into the front-passenger seat, my preferred spot in any cab or ride-share. As we drove through the city streets, chatting easily, the sights and sounds of Amman blurred together and I don't recall single word of what was said. Most likely, it was about local attractions in Amman or the historical city of Petra, after all, he was a tour company driver. But it didn't matter, I wasn't there to sightsee. I was just passing through.

Relatively quickly, almost too quickly, we arrived at the airport. Thanking my driver, I stepped out of the car and slung my backpack over my shoulder. Shielding my eyes against the rising morning sun with my left hand, I looked up at the sign above the airport, as if to reconfirm I was in the right spot. Or perhaps it was to steel myself for what was to come, a last look at a country at peace before flying into the unknown. Exhaling, I pushed my way into the airport and followed the signs to the military side of the sprawling complex. And finally, with a great sense of relief at no longer being alone, I found the other Americans who would be on the C-130 to Baghdad with me that day. They were lounging in a designated waiting area doing the various things that are done to pass time in an airport. Glancing around, I saw some were reading, others were listening to music on their iPods trying not to look anxious or nervous, and some were strewn across multiple airport seats, or simply lying on the ground, using their backpacks as pillows, and catching some much-needed sleep. We were a mix of folks flying together that day: State Department employees, military personnel, and military contractors. Making my way over to another individual who I assumed was a State Department employee, based on his civilian clothing choices and nonbuzz cut hair style, I introduced myself. I never asked this individual if I could include him in my book, so I'll just call him Joe. It was also Joe's first time flying to Baghdad. Chatting, we helped each other pass the time and keep our anxiety in check. He was a Schedule C State Department employee whose sarcasm and wit kept me laughing and distracted before the flight.

State Department Side Note: Like other executive branches, the State Department has both career employees and politically appointed employees. There are four main types of political appointed employees:

Presidential appointments with Senate confirmation: Cabinet-level positions and Ambassadors.

Presidential appointments without Senate confirmation: Likely senior positions within the Executive Office of the President.

Noncareer Senior Executive Service: The Senior Executive Service is the layer of management just below presidential appointments with Senate confirmation. Typically, they are career staff, but about 10 percent may be political appointees or Noncareer Senior Executive Service.

Schedule C: These jobs are usually lower-level political appointments. Basically, a way for relatives of sitting Senators, House members, other party-affiliated individuals to have jobs within the Executive Branch. I don't think Schedule C employees typically serve overseas, but Baghdad had a number of them, particularly in the Public Affairs Section. They worked with the press to help control the U.S. war narrative.

After what felt like endless waiting and lines and more waiting, and flight briefings and being assigned a required helmet and flak jacket in the Amman airport, Joe and I finally made our way, along with the others on our flight, single file, out to the tarmac and walked up the ramp of the C-130. Unlike commercial airplanes, where you board though a side door, C-130s have a back end that opens up, providing a large loading ramp for people and supplies. Attempting to calm myself, I took several deep breaths as I stepped aboard. Parading in and taking the next open seat behind the person in front of me, I quickly belted myself in, leaned my helmet-clad head back, and closed my eyes.

Inside a C-130, with seats folded up.

I had been briefed back in DC, and again in Amman, Jordan that flying in and out of Baghdad International Airport (BIAP) meant an uncomfortable trip in a windowless, air-conditionless, loud, military transport plane— where I'd sit knee to knee, literally, with the people on either side and across from me. On a full C-130 flight, passengers sit in four rows perpendicular to the pilot. The two outside rows sit with their backs against the plane, facing the middle of the C-130, while the two middle rows sit back-to-back facing the outside rows across from them. I'd also been told to expect a corkscrew landing, meaning quick drops in altitude, nose-diving descents, and rotating, basic maneuvers to minimize the risk of being shot down.

Luckily, by virtue of my place in line, I managed to get a seat against the wall of the plane, so I was able to lean my head back, taking pressure off my neck which was unaccustomed to the extra weight of the helmet. If I had had a seat in one of the two middle rows, leaning my head back would have meant crashing it into the person sitting back-to-back with me. Like most military gear, C-130s are not built for passenger comfort, they are built for maximum efficiency. Wearing a helmet and flak jacket is already an uncomfortable proposition. Wearing them, while harnessed into folding C-130 chairs, trying to retain a semblance of personal space while touching shoulders with the people on either side of you and knees with the person across from you can be downright claustrophobic. Not to mention that C-130s are not temperature controlled. Packed in like sardines, wearing our protective gear, I went from sweating profusely while sitting inside the plane on the hot Jordanian tarmac, to shivering, as the sweat turned cold once we took off and reached altitude. The loud roaring of the engines also meant I could no longer talk to Joe, so I kept my eyes closed and willed the time to pass quickly, but not too quickly. I was afraid of the descent and the possibility that our plane could be shot at by insurgents in Baghdad, as we attempted to land. Prone to motion sickness, I worried and wondered, without much hope, if the military provided in-seat barf bags like on commercial flights.

The flight flew by faster than I thought possible and thankfully the landing wasn't as bad as I feared. Apparently, it was a quiet day in Baghdad. We made a couple of quick drops in altitude, but there was no spiraling or rotating.

Once on the ground, I deboarded and was herded along to a waiting room, specifically designated for civilian government employees. Joe and I, and the other State Department employees among us, were told to sit tight, relax, watch a little TV, and wait for our ride to the Green Zone. The Green Zone was where the majority of noncombatant military personnel, State Department officers, and representatives from other government agencies were housed in Baghdad. Confused about the ride that we were waiting for, I didn't remember being briefed in Washington about the specifics, I asked my fellow State Department travelers—some of whom had been in and out of Baghdad previously—for more information.

I was told, for those unable to make VIP arrangements (like me and Joe), the only transportation option from BIAP to the Green Zone (and vice versa) was a bus, a.k.a. the Rhino Runner—Rhino for short (VIPs could potentially grab a seat on a helicopter or perhaps in an armored car). The Rhino was a heavily fortified boxy-military bus, capable of withstanding bullets and suicide bombers—at least that was the hope.

Here, I'm posing with a Rhino in Baghdad's Green Zone in fall of 2005.

Side view of a Rhino.

After explaining about the Rhino, the seasoned State Department Employee told me that on November 27, 2004, a car bomb with 250 pounds of explosives detonated six feet from a Rhino, creating a six-feet diameter crater and a 1,000-feet-long dust cloud. Thankfully, all the Rhino passengers survived. I anxiously wondered if the outcome would have been different had the bomb detonated right next to or under the Rhino instead of half-a-dozen feet away. I also wondered why my co-worker felt compelled to tell me about the bomb, right before my first Rhino ride? What is it with people, seriously? It reminds me of when I was pregnant with my first child and how other moms felt the need to tell me horror stories about pregnancy and child-birth. First-time mothers are already worried enough, they don't need to hear about your friend's sister's cousin's baby who needed an emergency C-section.

For security purposes, the military unit that operated the Rhino never posted its scheduled departure time in advance. It was likely to leave some-time during the middle of the night or in the early morning hours before dawn. Stress the *likely*. High levels of insurgent activity on the road, which was monitored by helicopters, could happen at any time (although less often at night), and could cause Rhino runs to be cancelled, delaying subsequent travel plans. Even though the Rhino was built to withstand a car bomb and keep running or at least prevent anyone from being killed, no one cared to test the statistics if it could be avoided.

After hours of waiting that first day at the Baghdad airport, we were finally told it was "go-time" and we were hustled onto the Rhino. And when I say hustled, I really mean *hustled* (I totally get that military hurry-up and wait cliché thing now). There was no room for lollygagging—helmet on (*check*), flak jacket on and buckled (*check*), heart palpitations (*check*). Some military dude standing by the Rhino door, waving his arm in a circular motion, screaming, "Let's go, let's go, let's go people!" (check). Obeying, I furiously clambered aboard, and followed the person in front of me. We loaded the bus back to front. Finding the first available seat, I slid into it as quickly as I could and sat in silent darkness praying there'd be no insurgent activity that night. Thinking back to the 2004 Rhino incident, I closed my eyes and calmed myself by silently repeating the mantra: *they took a bomb and survived, they took a bomb and survived, they took a bomb and survived.*

Rhino loaded, I held my breath in anticipation of our departure and fear that activity on the road would cause the ride to be cancelled. On that day, by luck, we were off. The military driver fired up the engine and sped away as quickly as possible to the Green Zone. The road from the airport to the Green Zone was a mere 7.5 miles long. However, Route Irish, as it was affectionately named by the American troops, was the world's most dangerous road at the time due to the high level of attacks on foreigners. No person without a death wish drove on it, unless it couldn't be avoided. I barely remembered to breathe.

Side note: I'm not sure why the U.S. Military called the airport road "Route Irish." One clever Internet user surmised it might be because it led to the "Green Zone," and green is often associated with Ireland.

For the entire 7.5 miles, there was an overabundance of adrenaline racing through my body, and I couldn't to do a damn thing but sit tight and will the ride to be over. Riding in the Rhino was nothing like any of the previous bus rides I'd been on before. Not only did it lack cushioned seats and hand bars, standard for city buses that I was accustomed to (Rhinos were purely a functional bus meant for strength and durability, with little thought for passenger comfort)—the physical and emotional responses I experienced did not compare to previous bus rides I had been on. While it's true, there have been times that I felt like I could die on a city bus ride, the logical part of my brain always knew it was extremely unlikely. When riding a Rhino, however, my rational mind knew death was a real possibility.

Normally when I feel sick or uncomfortable on a moving vehicle, I stare out the window. But I couldn't even do that—Rhinos have little, tiny windows that are up too high—the only way to peer out of them was by standing up.

Exhaling and letting the adrenaline seep out of me, we finally arrived in the Green Zone at 3 a.m. My body felt done. After two or three days traveling from Washington, DC, I'd lost count of the hours, made more complicated by the multiple time zone changes. Heavy with exhaustion and discombobulated by my overworked adrenal glands, I barely had the emotional and physical energy for first impressions as I stepped off the Rhino. Collecting my backpack that had been stowed on the bus, and slinging it over one shoulder, I looked around for the first time at what was to be my home for the year. I felt like I'd been deposited in a post-apocalyptic, military-chic, bus depot. I was unsure of what I was supposed to do next. Thankfully, before I had time to really contemplate my next more, the Consul General found me. The top official of my new department, he introduced himself, holding out his hand and saying, "You must be Amy. Hi. I'm Richard, but you can call me Dick.

Welcome to the Green Zone." (My inner child suppressed a giggle every time I witnessed him meeting someone new who called him Richard. With a straight, deadpan face, he'd say every time, "You can call me Dick.")

After welcoming me, Dick said, "I picked up your trailer key today. Are you ready to walk over to it?" Glancing around, checking to make sure there wasn't some other military check-out process or procedure that needed to be completed, I waved to Joe and turning back to Dick I said, "I'm ready" with more enthusiasm than I felt.

Together, we walked the quarter-mile or so from the Rhino stop to the former palace grounds of Saddam Hussein, where most Americans in the Green Zone were housed. We likely engaged in small-talk along the way, but I was too drained to remember anything that was said.

Entering through the remnants of Palace gates, Dick and I made our way to my trailer park. There were at least a half-dozen separate trailer parks set up around the Palace, the cafeteria, and the massive American military gym. Passing several rows of tan trailers, separated by sandbags, Dick took a right and walked to the middle of one row. Stopping outside my trailer, he handed me my key and said, "I'll be back at 8 a.m. to take you to the DFAC (military cafeteria) and then to the office." Murmuring, "thank you," I unlocked my door and stepped inside. My new home was a converted shipping container. It was big enough for a single bed, a small armoire (which sounds fancier than it really was), a small writing desk, one chair, and a TV. I had a shared bathroom with another woman whose trailer butted up to mine.

Letting my backpack slip off my shoulder and on to the ground with a plunk, exhausted, I fell face down on my bed, and went to sleep—helmet and dust-covered shoes, still on.

I later learned having my own, single trailer was living the high-life, compared to the military. Soon after my arrival, I became friends with a fellow Midwesterner and military reservist. We, who are considered to be from the flyover zone, are often automatically bonded by the geography of our upbringing. And I think some of the military reservists felt they could relate more with the civilian employees (like me) than with career military personnel. I met a number of reservists who had signed up for the reserves for the education perks, playing Army one or two weekends a month—but otherwise living the life of a civilian with a career, a family, a community. One woman had been working as a geologist for over twenty years for the State of Pennsylvania. Then when the war happened, and the Defense Department needed bodies, the reservists were called up—leaving behind their jobs as geologists and managers and dentists and doctors and lawyers (there were all of the above)—to serve their country in the Green Zone, usually performing a job completely unrelated to the careers they been pursuing for the past ten or twenty years. They were in a strange limbo-land, technically part of the military, but mentally often not.

The reservist invited me to his trailer to play cards with him and his roommates. That's when I realized they had to cram two to four people in a similarly sized container to mine. And their bathrooms were in another separate trailer that they had to walk to. They never complained about the disparity, but I definitely felt like the upper class, but not necessarily in a good way. I hadn't done anything to earn the special treatment; it had been handed to me simply because of my employer.

Here is the walkway to my trailer.

This is the inside of my trailer—
the picture makes it look larger than reality.

CHAPTER 7:

Women in the Workplace, in the Foreign Service, in Baghdad

Before describing my arrival and first day in Baghdad further, I'm going to step back and try to explain how being a woman impacted my experience in the workplace, as a Foreign Service Officer and, more specifically, as a female Foreign Service Officer in a war zone. This chapter has been the most difficult for me to write. Not because of the content, but I've struggled with *how* to put my thoughts into words. Like most women I know, I am cognizant of my surroundings and attuned to potential threats from men, regardless of where I am and what I am doing, whether jogging in the local park or the brisk walk to my car after an evening grocery shopping trip. This natural danger radar multiplied by 1,000 when I worked in a war zone predominantly staffed by men, and impacted my psyche in ways I have yet to completely confront or understand.

I remember when I was eighteen and starting college, all incoming first-year students were gathered into a large auditorium, against our wishes, to talk about Campus Safety and Security. Our thoughts were focused on meeting new friends, the weekend party we'd heard about, and just stretching our wings now that we were no longer under parental control. Discussing campus safety and security was the last thing on our minds.

Amidst the jostling, the chatter, the squeak of auditorium seating, and the wisecracks by eighteen-year-old knuckleheads, we learned not only the campus safety rules but also tips for "the girls" to reduce their chances of "becoming a victim," a.k.a. how *not* to get raped on campus. All very sensible suggestions, "Do not wear a ponytail when walking alone, especially at night, as it gives someone behind you something to grab onto." "Do not walk alone at night, full-stop, especially through the park." "Do not attend a party on your own, make sure to always go with a group of friends who can keep an eye on you."

"Sometimes being a girl really sucks," I thought to myself. "I shouldn't need a group of friends or a male escort to protect me. I should be able to walk around alone, like the guys apparently can, without having to worry that someone is going to violate me." It didn't make sense to me. I resented the notion that being a girl meant I had to always be vigilant for would-be attackers to jump out from behind the bushes or accost me if I let loose and had one drink too many.

For better or for worse, that campus security seminar stuck with me and life experiences have taught me, despite my resentment, that in reality it actually was the best, easier even, to have a man on hand for protection. The trouble is, it can't just be any man; it has to be the *right* man. Sometimes, our better judgment fails us and men we dismiss as nonthreatening, or as friends, can take us by surprise and hurt us. It is with lived experience, that just being female means I come with built-in vulnerabilities, that I entered the Foreign Service.

Saying that the State Department is deeply traditional, hierarchical, and bureaucratic is an understatement. Compared to the relative informality of the private sector, stepping into the halls of the State Department often made me feel that I was being transported back to days gone by. The dress code is business. I wore a suit every day, until I went to Baghdad. When serving overseas, all Foreign Service Personnel stand when the Ambassador walks into the room, no one leaves a diplomatic function if the Ambassador is still present, and there are protocols about who occupies what seat in a car. All employees are constantly aware of rank and seniority. And historically, the Foreign Service has been very traditional and slow to enter the modern world.

Women Foreign Service Officers did not have the right to be Foreign Service Officers *and* be married, until the 1970s. Before that, women had to quit the Foreign Service if they decided to marry. Then came Alison Palmer. Alison filed the first equal employment opportunity (EEO) complaint against the State Department in 1968. She won her case in 1971, following which the State Department made several important changes on behalf of women officers, including allowing them to be married.

Today, it is more difficult for female Foreign Service Officers to find a spouse willing to follow them around the world, compared to male officers; however, this may have nothing to do with Foreign Service regulations but may simply be a reflection of our culture.

On one hand, while part of me wishes that I was born thirty years earlier, so I could have been a hippie in San Francisco in the 1960s, another part of me feels fortunate that I wasn't born until the 1970s. Multiple generations of women, starting with Lucile Atcherson in 1922, served in the Foreign Service before me, paving the way for me and other women. My road was not as tough as theirs. I never had to deal with men slapping me on the rear end as I walked past, well except for one time when I was a *Perkins'* server during college. But even then, because of the women that came before me, I had the power to kick the offender out of the restaurant and tell him he was never allowed to come back again. I didn't just have to take it.

I was only in the Foreign Service for six years. I loved every minute (almost) and would have gladly continued to serve, but life pulled me in another direction and I couldn't bend the bureaucracy to fit my circumstances, so I had no choice but to quit. During those six years, I was posted exclusively to the Middle East and North Africa.

I'm frequently asked, "How did Middle Eastern men treat you? Were they OK working with a woman?"

My response, "It was never a problem. Male officials in the Middle East were never anything but respectful to me."

I did have a couple of run-ins with Middle Eastern men, but never in an official capacity. Once, while shopping with an American friend in a crowded Tunisian outdoor market, I heard the guttural sound of someone working up a good glob of spit next to me. As I turned to investigate the noise, to my surprise I was hit with a big wad of it right in my face and chest—so gross. To this day, I don't think being spat at had to do with my gender, I think being an American was enough to warrant the spittle. Other than being momentarily taken aback and *really* disgusted, it didn't register as that big a deal to me. My friend handed me a tissue, which I used to wipe myself off as best I could and we continued shopping. The truth is, I pity the spitter. He was probably just trying to express his political opinion and disdain for the United States. And yet, there's a good chance he's rotting away in a Tunisian prison somewhere, literally. At the time, Tunisia had one of the highest, if not the highest, ratios of police to civilians in the world. The place was littered with undercover cops. It's pretty likely the guy was hauled off the minute it happened. And according to reports I'd heard from our Political Officer, prisons in Tunisia were not a nice place to be.

Another time in Tunis, a female friend and I were walking home after an early evening cigarette run to a small, local corner market, the kind of place that sells beverages, cigarettes, and junk food. The sun had just set, so we were hurrying up the hill, before it got completely dark, especially as we knew our street lamp was broken. When, out of the corner of our eyes, we saw a random Tunisian guy pick up a couple of loose paving stones from the side of the road, which he proceeded to throw at us. As the first flew by, the edge of it managed to scrape my friend's head. Her forehead bleeding, we tried to run away, weaving between the parked cars along the side of the road to reduce the chances of being hit by the onslaught. Then, out of stones and faster than he looked, he ran up to us and grabbed one of my arms with both of his hands and started dragging me back down the street in the direction from which we had come. My free arm flailing, I tried to make contact with his face or body, but he was quite tall and lanky and I couldn't reach. My attempts to make myself heavy, so he couldn't drag me along like a rag doll, also failed.

Again, I don't think the attack had to do with my gender or this time even my nationality. I later found out this particular man was known to the local cops. He'd been diagnosed with a severe mental illness and had been institutionalized, but had apparently escaped—again. It's unclear what was going through his head when he attacked me and my friend.

Luckily, a quick-thinking high-school kid, exiting a school that just happened to be across the street from where we were, saved us. He, without hesitation, ran up and distracted our attacker by furiously swinging his backpack at my would-be kidnapper's face and chest, allowing me to pull my arm free and run home with my friend. We called the Regional Security Officer (RSO) and reported the incident. The RSO came and took our statements, made sure we were all right, and liaised with the local police—incident handled. My friend's head wound turned out to be pretty minor, so a Band-Aid and a glass of wine later, we felt better. My only regret is that I never met or had the opportunity to thank our high-school hero.

Side Note: Foreign Service Officers are considered "generalists," mean-
ing that regardless of your assigned cone, Political, Economic, Public Affairs,
Management, or Consular, you can be called upon to fulfill any of the five offi-
cer functions. In addition to Foreign Service Generalists, there are also Foreign
Service "Specialists." Regardless of where they are posted, specialists have the
one job, they are the computer technicians, the medical staff, and the security
specialists. Depending on the size of the embassy or consulate, each has a given
number of Assistant Regional Security Officers (ARSOs) and a head Regional
Security Officer (RSO). Anything and everything that have to do with person-
nel or property, safety and security, goes through the RSO office. They are like
the internal State Department police.

The only time it ever felt like a Middle Eastern man even acknowl-
edged my gender, in an official capacity, was pretty hilarious. It was when I
was in Libya. I was in an opulent hotel, wearing my suit and pearls and having
dinner with two men: a Tunisian businessman and a longtime Libyan oil field
worker. I was trying to understand and learn about the business climate and
opportunities for American oil companies in Libya. In my twenties, anyone
over forty seemed pretty ancient to me. So, while I can't say for sure, I think
the Libyan oil hand was in his mid-to-late fifties and he had an altogether
disheveled appearance. His hair was thinning and sticking up in all different
directions from his head, and he was also noticeably missing a couple of teeth.
As we sat down to dinner, scooting our chairs up to the table, the first thing
he said to me was, "I'm happy to tell you everything I know about working
in Libya's oil fields, but I have to warn you, whatever you do, *do not* fall in
love with me." The three of us chuckled pretty heartily, the ice was broken,
and the meeting carried on comfortably.

In general, being a female American diplomat in the Middle East was
an asset. The Middle Eastern men I encountered went out of their way to
be helpful, respectful, and courteous. It was almost as if they felt like they
needed to take care of me, introduce me to the "right" people, and assist me
in getting the information I needed. This ultimately meant that I was granted

access and details that were sometimes not accessible to my male colleagues. If the gentleman I was meeting with couldn't answer my questions, it was common to hear, "I don't know the answer. But you should meet Mohamed, he can help you. Let me call him for you right now."

Regarding my male American colleagues, however, respectful is not a term that always applied. To be clear, 99.9 percent of my interactions with my male counterparts were fine, good even. However, every once in a while, my gender was very much front and center in a way that I did not or still would not welcome in the workplace. And any incident, is one incident too many.

Tunis, being on the Mediterranean, was a port of call for NATO ships. Once, when a NATO ship came to port in Tunisia, our U.S. Naval Attaché wanted to show the visiting soldiers a good time. He walked around the U.S. Embassy offices, only inviting the single American women to a party aboard the ship that evening. If I'm honest, I knew he was totally pimping us out, but in that instance, I didn't really mind. I thought it was a great opportunity to see what it was like aboard a NATO ship, an opportunity not afforded to my male colleagues or to the married women. And I thought to myself, "just because I'm invited to the party, doesn't mean I have to spend the night with any sailors afterwards."

Aboard a NATO ship.

One instance when I very much *did mind* a male colleague's attention took place in Libya, when a handful of us were living in the Corinthia Hotel in Tripoli. While the highest-ranking member of our team, whom I shall call Bob, was frequently traveling back and forth to Washington, when Bob was in town, his assigned hotel room was right next to mine. In fact, our headboards shared the same wall.

Given that we had no office space beyond the hotel, my room served as both my bedroom and my office. In addition to two beds, it had a wooden desk tucked against one wall and a round café table with two chairs next to a large set of windows. I often held meetings at the café table with the other State Department staff to avoid prying eyes from the locals or other foreigners in the lobby. As the premier establishment for visiting Westerners, the Corinthia's lobby was no doubt also crawling with Libyan secret police.

One day, Bob and I were meeting at the café table in my room. Dressed in business attire, legs crossed, sipping coffee, and munching on a shared bowl of pistachios, we discussed my upcoming meetings and the information I still needed to complete my work on the Country Commercial Guide. I had some papers on the table in front of me and was pointing at a few interesting facts that I didn't want to say out loud, as my room was no doubt bugged with listening devices. We were the first American State Department employees in Libya in a long time, so of course the Libyan Government wanted to keep a close eye on what we were doing.

Then unexpectedly, right in the middle of me explaining something, he interrupted. I looked up, unable to interpret his look, or at least not wanting to believe it. In the same matter-of-fact business tone, he'd been using to go over my work, he said, "Amy, there's something I've been wanting to tell you that's really been bothering me…Just knowing that my bedroom is right on the other side of yours and that our headboards share the same wall is driving me crazy. I've been tossing and turning at night and I haven't been sleeping well. I keep envisioning you right on the other side of the wall from me, asleep in your bed. Sometimes I get so excited by the thought of you sleeping so close, yet just out of reach, that I feel like I could scratch down the wall between us with my bare hands to get to you."

My first thought to his confession was, "What the fuck, dude?!? Seriously. What am I supposed to do with this? Number one, let's be honest, I'm not attracted to your dowdy old ass *at all*, but even if I was, it is *completely* unfair of you to put me in this position—to do this to me or say this to me. I am a *first tour* officer. You are a *senior* officer! I'm trying to be a professional here and establish my reputation and my good name, and you have to go and act like some creepy, gross old guy—ugh! What do I say in this situation? And who can I even report this behavior to? You are the most senior person at our mission, and we don't have any security or human resources officers here yet. I'm sure my male colleagues don't have to put up with this shit from you. This sucks. You suck. And this is all so inappropriate."

I am a conflict avoider. It's something I am working on and getting better at. But, at the time, it was extremely difficult for me to engage in uncomfortable conversations, without making excuses for others, or stumbling over my words, or simply crying.

I just stared at Bob for a minute with a disgusted look on my face, like I had smelled a skunk. I think it was enough for him to understand that I was not the least bit interested in whatever sick, twisted fantasy was going on in his perverted mind. Thank goodness, he didn't try anything physical. Although, if he had, to be honest, I think I could have taken him. Apologizing, I made up an excuse that he needed to leave because I had a lunch meeting to go to. Only now do I realize that I went out of my way to make the environment more comfortable for *him* after *he* had behaved so inappropriately. He should have been the one trying to make me feel more comfortable, or apologized—not the other way around. After that, he only asked for a private meeting in my room one other time, but I declined and suggested we meet in a public space instead.

Recalling the lessons of my first-year college safety seminar, I found myself a local boyfriend for the remainder of my stay in Libya. We had met in the hotel lobby, as he frequently came to use the hotel gym. He was young and cute and stayed over whenever Bob was in town. Born in Libya, but a British citizen, he'd recently moved to Tripoli from the UK to be on the front end of what he hoped would be a booming economy with the Americans moving in. I don't recall thinking that I needed a boyfriend for protection, but looking back, the timing seemed like too much of a coincidence for that not to be the case, even if subconsciously.

My encounter with Bob in Libya was unfortunately neither my first nor my last inappropriate interaction with a male colleague while working for the

State Department. But it particularly stands out because there was no system in place to address the inappropriateness of it all. Granted, it was an unusual situation with just a handful of us Foreign Service Officers and two computer techs, living and working out of a hotel, with none of the standard reporting chains and bureaucracy in place. The fact however that Bob, my superior, confided his sexual fantasies to me in my hotel room, particularly given the power differential between us, was shocking to me. It was the twenty-first century; everyone had plenty of sexual harassment training at that point. I can't begin to imagine what was going on in his head, why he thought such behavior was OK, or what sort of reaction he expected from me.

Having first-hand experience with workplace harassment in multiple non-war zones, where there were equitable numbers of males and females, I was extremely trepidatious about walking into the male-dominated environment of Baghdad's Green Zone. I'd heard from women who served in Baghdad before me that the Green Zone was almost all male, with testosterone-laden men at that, and that I should expect "a lot of attention." As I nervously flew into Baghdad on the C-130, a big part of me was scared about the danger of living someplace where gunfire and bombings were common. A smaller, but still present, part of me, was concerned about my safety from my future male colleagues and employees of the Department of Defense. I hoped that my female colleagues exaggerated what was to come.

They had not. Being a woman in the Green Zone, in 2005, was like being an exotic animal on display at a zoo. My clothing choices quickly changed—the skirts stayed in the closet and I dressed more androgynously, not showing cleavage or curves in public, not that it made much difference. My public demeanor also adapted to the environment relatively quickly. Pre-Iraq, I was friendly and outgoing, often greeting strangers when out walking. In the Green Zone, I learned it was the easiest to wear sunglasses and headphones at all times—that way no one could catch my eye and think I wanted to interact with them. An errant smile was interpreted as more than a smile; it was seen as an invitation for unwelcomed behavior. Once, I remember two young soldiers trying to talk to me and get my attention as I walked past. Ignoring them and pretending I couldn't hear behind my headphones, I heard one of them say to his friend, "It's true what they say, all the hot ones are bitches." In my mind, I nodded along, thinking, "That's right buddy, I'm a bitch, so just keep walkin.'"

As if the daily catcalls and looks and feeling like I was constantly on display wasn't enough, less than a month after arriving in Baghdad, I received an unwelcomed email—on my official State Department email account—from an Assistant Regional Security Officer (ARSO). Yes, the individuals who are charged with keeping the rest of State Department employees safe.

I had been to one of the Green Zone bars the night before and someone told this ARSO about me. And apparently, he thought I would welcome an email from him, a complete stranger to me, commenting on my attractiveness. He thought such an email would "brighten" my day.

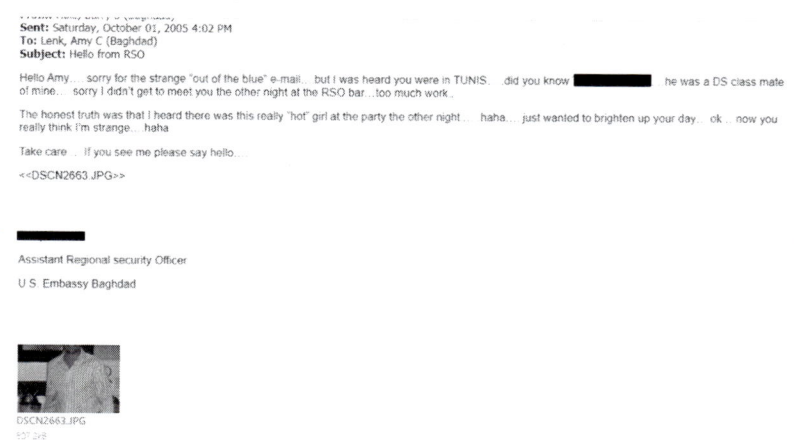

Sent: Saturday, October 01, 2005 4:02 PM
To: Lenk, Amy C (Baghdad)
Subject: Hello from RSO

Hello Amy... sorry for the strange "out of the blue" e-mail... but I was heard you were in TUNIS... did you know ▇▇▇▇▇▇ he was a DS class mate of mine... sorry I didn't get to meet you the other night at the RSO bar...too much work .

The honest truth was that I heard there was this really "hot" girl at the party the other night ... haha... just wanted to brighten up your day... ok ... now you really think I'm strange... haha

Take care .. if you see me please say hello...

<<DSCN2663.JPG>>

▇▇▇▇▇▇
Assistant Regional security Officer
U.S. Embassy Baghdad

DSCN2663.JPG

Opening the email, my first thought was, "Wait, what the?!? How am I supposed to trust these guys with my safety and security, if they start harassing me over email? I obviously can't ever go to this guy with any personal security concerns now, it would be too awkward. And not only can I not trust him, I wonder who else was gossiping about me?"

Next, I thought, "Boy this guy is dumb. If he's going to send harassing emails, he should probably use a personal email address, not his state.gov account! I mean come on. Also, what is with the attached body shot photo?"

I ended up not responding and instead forwarded the email to Dick and said it made me uncomfortable and that I didn't appreciate receiving harassing messages from the RSO office. I'm not sure what happened from there. Honestly, I don't think anything ever came of it. I just searched for the guy while writing this and he's still at State, receiving awards for his exemplary service. At the end of the day, apparently it didn't matter that he'd harassed a colleague via his work email account. In the list of war zone priorities, using official government email to send female colleagues pictures of yourself and talk about how hot they were, likely did not rate as important. My concern for my safety felt totally irrelevant.

Frankly, I was not surprised my complaint was not taken seriously. Precedent is set from the top. And soon after I arrived in Baghdad, more than one State Department female colleague told me, "Watch out for [name removed], he can get a little 'handsy' if you know what I mean." Fortunately, I was low enough in the chain of command that the particular senior official the women were referring to was easy for me avoid. I was only in his proximity once. He made an appearance at one of the Baghdad bars on a Friday night when I was there and suggested we pose for a picture together. Positioned right next to him, he caressed the side of my breast. After the photo-op, I fumed, "Do my male colleagues have to deal with this shit? Why is this OK? Why does this senior official think it's OK to touch the breast of a junior female colleague?" And apparently, he's done it enough that his reputation preceded him. Multiple women warned me about his behavior. It made me wonder what else he was up to, but glad whatever it was that I wasn't involved.

Like everywhere else, workplace harassment obviously also happens in the State Department and is potentially made worse by the traditional, hierarchical culture that often makes junior officers feel powerless against their more senior colleagues. And it isn't always men harassing women it can happen the other way as well. I once knew a single, senior female officer who, when drunk, would try to get the young Marine Security Guards to go home with her. I'm sure it wasn't very comfortable for them either.

Being a woman has always shaped my feeling of security, or lack thereof. I was already cognizant of the dangers of being alone at night in parks or in parking garages before going to Baghdad. Added to this general situational awareness, in Iraq, there was the reality of living predominantly among men. And my experiences quickly made me feel that confronting harassment of me, and other women, was a nonpriority in a war zone—or just another casualty of war. Our complaints were not heard. Not only did bombings and bullets become a part of everyday life, so too did catcalls and ogling.

CHAPTER 8:

The Consular Staff

Back to my first day in Baghdad. As promised, there was a crisp knock on my door a few hours after Dick had escorted me to my trailer. I was ready and waiting. I'd gotten up thirty minutes earlier and taken a shower and dressed. Shrugging my shoulders, a couple of times, and twisting my head from left to right I opened the door. My neck and back were stiff from wearing the flak jacket and helmet for most of the day before—they were an uncomfortable addition that I was not accustomed to and luckily did not need to use on a regular basis. We were supposed to wear them more often than we did.

Dick was ready to take me to the DFAC (military dining facility) for breakfast, which was about a five-minute walk from my new quarters. Stepping outside, I pivoted halfway around to lock the door, and as I turned back, I was able to assess my surroundings for the first time in the morning light. The air already felt heavy with the heat and humidity to come, and I was struck by its yellowness, laden with dust. Average temperatures in Baghdad in the late summer are well over 100 degrees Fahrenheit. As we left the trailer park, I noticed large vats of individual water bottles, which Dick said were free to grab whenever anyone needed one. He said that dehydration in Baghdad's oppressive hot weather was common if people didn't drink enough water. As we rounded the corner, as my tour guide, he pointed out the laundry trailer I could use at my leisure. Entering what appeared to a main thoroughfare, I looked to my right and saw behind an iron fence, that there were multiple toppled and defaced statues—the remnants of the Saddam era.

Defaced Statue

Not able to take in the sights and sounds around me quickly enough, we soon arrived at the DFAC, which fed the thousands of soldiers and civilian government staff living and working near the Republican Palace—Saddam's former palatial residence that served as an office building for the majority of the U.S. Military and civilian workforce in the Green Zone.

The first thing I spotted as we approached the DFAC were signs instructing individuals to clear their weapons of ammunition before stepping inside, via the multiple large barrels tipped at forty-five-degree angles with holes in the top and surrounded by sandbags. "Huh, I have not seen that before on an overseas tour," I thought to myself, wondering how many more times I would think that before the day was done.

Before Baghdad, my interactions with the military were primarily limited to several multi-day trips, when I worked in Tunisia and Bahrain. Once in Tunisia, the U.S. Ambassador flew on a small U.S. Military plane down to the southernmost tip of the country, deep in the desert. He was to tour an oil field and engage in some general goodwill activities with the host nation (meeting the local police, riding a camel, etc.). As the Economic Officer, I was assigned to travel with him to take notes on the trip. During the excursion, we spent one night at a hotel. The military personnel that accompanied us (as it was a military transport plane) told me to be in the lobby the next morning at 8 a.m. for our departure. My parents had instilled the importance of being punctual at an early age, so I stepped into the lobby at exactly 8 a.m., only to see that I was the last one to arrive. Later, one of the military officers pulled me aside and in an admonishing tone said, "Amy, why were you late this morning? You are the most junior person here and you kept everyone waiting!"

Slightly put off by his scolding, I was not after all in his chain of command, I retorted, "You told me to be in the lobby at 8 a.m., and I was, I don't understand how that is late!?"

He continued, "When I said 8 a.m., I thought you knew you should always report at least fifteen minutes earlier, especially as a junior officer."

Realizing that we were in the middle of a culture clash, but cranky from a lack of caffeine and not wanting to concede any ground, I snapped back, "Next time, if you want me to be someplace at 7:45, then tell me 7:45 and I will be there, don't give me a time fifteen minutes after I'm supposed to arrive." Both of us a bit worked up, we left it at that and turned and walked away from each other.

Stepping through the DFAC doors for the first time in Baghdad, I remembered back to that culture clash in Tunisia. Everything felt kind of hazy or foggy at first, it was difficult to focus and take it all in. The jet lag was partially to blame, but it was also the newness of it all. Military life was an unknown entity to me, and the gymnasium-sized DFAC, packed with soldiers in camo and lots of guns, felt like a foreign land where I didn't quite understand the rules and didn't quite look the part. My baby-blue short-sleeved button-down dress shirt and tailored dress pants stood out among the sea of desert camo.

As I scanned the room, it felt like hundreds of pairs of eyes turned and stared right back at me; as mentioned, civilian American women were few and far between in the Green Zone. I'd been told to expect roughly a 90:10 or 95:5 ratio of men to women (I'm not sure if that figure was accurate, I never counted). But I hadn't anticipated how unsettling the gender disparity would be.

Not wanting to be the object of the men's scrutiny any longer than necessary, I made a beeline to the first buffet table I saw and grabbed a hard-boiled egg. After finding the beverage station and filling up a cup of coffee, I spotted Dick and we grabbed a couple of open seats. Needless to say, I was a little nervous about my first day on the job and somewhat unnerved by the staring, and unable to completely let my guard down because I was break-fasting with my bosses' boss. I nibbled on my hard-boiled egg and gulped down the tepid coffee.

Dick was anxious to get his day started, so in relatively short order, we finished our meals, bused our plastic trays, and pushed our way back out the DFAC doors. Along the way, he informed me that while the Republican Palace housed most of the U.S. Government offices, including those of all other State Department staff, the Consular section was actually across the

Green Zone in a separate building that we shared with the U.S. Department of Agriculture and the U.S. Department of Commerce. It was the official U.S. Embassy and had been given to the U.S. Government by the new Iraqi Government. However, it was much too small to meet the U.S. Government's needs, so the majority of Americans worked in Saddam's former Republican Palace until construction of a new embassy building could begin.

As our office was across the Green Zone, and Baghdad could be unbearably hot making walking enormously uncomfortable, except in winter months, the American Consular staff were each assigned their own personal vehicles. Mine was not yet available, so I rode with Dick to our building.

The drive was not all that far, but it was slow going and took even longer because of the midway military checkpoint guarded by U.S. Marines and a second, more extensive vehicle screening necessary to enter the Embassy compound. Armed Gurkhas (Nepalese soldiers) inspected each vehicle entering the U.S. Embassy compound with bomb-sniffing dogs and long-handled mirrors able to view a vehicle's undercarriage. Individuals intent on harming U.S. interests were known to carry bomb parts into and around the Green Zone. Not necessarily completed bombs, but a few parts here and there that could be assembled. A guard told me that his dog once found a fuse hidden behind a headlight. Despite my probing, he refused to indulge my curiosity about who was smuggling bomb parts and what had happened to them.

Dick's vehicle checked, with a bow and a "Namaste," the guards waved us through. We parked and made our way up the marble steps and through the grand embassy entrance. Most embassies are guarded by a specialized Marine Security Guard Unit, but not the then U.S. Embassy in Baghdad. Marines guard embassies to protect classified U.S. Government materials, not U.S. Government employees. The Baghdad Embassy, as it only housed the Consular Section, the Department of Agriculture, and the Department of Commerce, did not contain any classified materials, and therefore Marines were not necessary. The Marines did guard Saddam's Palace, which is where classified information was held. At the embassy, a local guard was stationed at the entrance to double check that everyone entering and exiting had the appropriate blue badge.

Once inside, we headed down a flight of stairs to the Consular section's basement office. Walking through the doors for the first time, I was momentarily confused and almost took a step backwards. The gray cubicle walls and desks were exactly like my office at Prudential in Plymouth, Minnesota, and weren't what I expected to see in a war zone. Somehow, I figured conditions would be a little more dilapidated. Not quite bullet-ridden, but at least not have the sterile-corporate America feel of any generic office building.

Over-coming my momentary surprise, I smiled as my new coworkers stood up from their desks and walked over to meet Dick and me in the doorway. There was Dick's deputy, a longtime Consular Officer and my immediate supervisor, two other junior officers like myself who had arrived just a couple of weeks before and already seemed to have the routine down, and four Iraqi women, whom I shall call Asha, Nadira, Minna, and Sameen. While the Iraqis could not adjudicate visas or notarize documents like the rest of us, they were invaluable when it came to processing applications and providing translation services.

The women were diverse in background: Minna was a Kurd from Northern Iraq, Nadira was a Sunni Muslim, Asha was Christian, and I believe Sameen was a Shi'ite Muslim (although she could have also been Sunni, I'm not 100 percent sure). Despite the civil war raging outside, their backgrounds and religions didn't matter in the office or hadn't mattered until postwar factionalism surfaced. They often made the point that pre-second Gulf War, the religion of their neighbors had been inconsequential. However, in the new post-Saddam world, "outsiders" were capitalizing on the mayhem and stoking insurgencies with nationalist rhetoric. I placed outsiders in quotes because that's what the women claimed. They said that based on the accents of the insurgents, the worst of the bunch were most assuredly not Iraqis from Baghdad.

Religious Side Note: The original split between Sunni and Shi'ite Muslims happened in 632 after the death of the Prophet Mohammed. Sunnis wanted an elite group of community leaders to determine succession, while the Shi'ite preferred religious leadership remain within the Prophet's family. Despite this divide, the various Muslim factions have largely existed peacefully together in the absence of political leadership capitalizing on nationalism for its own gain. The Shi'ite regional stronghold is Iran, while Sunnis often receive support from Saudi Arabia. While the Shi'ite get a bad rap, likely due to their affiliation with Iran, big bad terrorist groups such as Al Qaeda and ISIS are Sunnis.

I immediately felt at home among my coworkers and, over time, my respect for the Iraqi staff grew immensely. As I got to know them and more about life in Baghdad, I realized they were risking their lives to come work with us each day. They did not have armed escorts to get them from their homes in the Red Zone into the Green Zone; they had to pass through insurgent strongholds and wait in long lines just to get to work each day. They all used assumed names in order to avoid being targeted by terrorists who hated the Iraqis who worked for America, almost as much as they hated the Americans. And despite their long and difficult commute, they showed up to work every day, surprisingly on time and performed their jobs admirably. They proudly told me that before the war, throughout the Middle East, Iraqi women were the closest to American or Western women in terms of the freedoms they were allowed including their level of education, and their ability to choose their type of employment. And, not only were they courageous, smart, and dedicated but also all very beautiful.

I often joked with them how regardless of the roving blackouts, limited water, unbearable heat, and annoyingly long and scary commutes into the Green Zone they always showed up dressed immaculately, perfectly coiffed, makeup intact. Then there was me, who had the luxury of air conditioning, a shower, constant electricity, and a short commute, but never wore anything fancier than wrinkled khakis. I didn't wear makeup. And I pulled my wet hair into a bun or ponytail so I didn't have to deal with it.

Although the Iraqi women never came right out and said it, they were too kind for that, I think they were slightly appalled at my lack of concern over my appearance. One morning, Nadira said to me, "Amy, I bought you something. It's not exactly what I was looking for, but it was the best I could do with the empty store shelves right now." I was immediately touched by her gesture, knowing she had risked going shopping for me in Baghdad. The streets in Baghdad were not safe. We received almost daily reports of car bombs and shootings. Our Iraqi staff would tell us morgues were so full, bodies were being piled up outside of them.

Needless to say, I was curious to see what she'd risk her safety to buy for me. And then, from behind her back, Nadira pulled out an eyeliner pencil. Beaming, she handed it to me saying, "I'm happy to give you lessons during our lunch break and teach you how to use it." Moved by her kindness, I willingly agreed even though I was not expecting much success. And she tried. Repeatedly. To teach me. Ultimately to no avail. I always smudged it or it would be too thick in some parts, or too thin in others. In the end, we just gave up. My make-up-free face could not be conquered by her well intentions.

The eyeliner wasn't the first or the last gift the Iraqi staff gave me. They were consistently generous and went out of their way to make our office a home away from home. Occasionally, they brought us Iraqi meals or treats they'd prepared. And, as they knew I didn't like to eat things with sugar, for my birthday, they bought me an assortment of fine cheeses and stuck a birthday candle in one.

I tried to reciprocate with gifts of my own; after all, I had access to online shopping and the military postal system. During a particularly hot stretch, when power outages were common, I gave each of them a small, battery-powered fan. They were showing up to work exhausted, unable to sleep due to the extreme heat and lack of air conditioning, which was impacting their work performance. Delighted with their fans, they proclaimed they would be able to sleep better. The next morning Asha told me, "I was getting a great night's sleep until my mom came into my room during the middle of the night and stole my fan!"

While I enjoyed working with all four women, I became particularly close to Asha. In fact, she and an American woman named Marla Ruzicka were each a major inspiration to me for writing this book and co-founding Undivided.

CHAPTER 9:

Asha's Story

When I met Asha, the first thing that struck me was her head of big, wild frizzy hair and her even bigger, brighter smile. Small in stature, she drew me in with her sunny personality. She was the first one I went to with my questions and we soon became close friends.

Like the rest of the Iraqi staff, she used an assumed name. Despite this added layer of protection, one Sunday afternoon after returning home from a long weekend in Northern Iraq, she found a note tacked to her front door that read: *[Insert Asha's real, full name] we know where you work and who you work for. If you return to work tomorrow, we will kill you and your family.*

To say that the message was unsettling would be an understatement. Asha called me in a panic, crying as she asked, "Amy, what do I do? I can't lose my job, but I can't put my family in danger either." She was much more concerned about her family members, than her own life.

I said, "I'm so sorry this happened to you. Just hold on please, we can figure this out. Let me talk to a few people and I'll call you back in an hour."

First, I called Dick to let him know what had happened. I said, "I'm going to talk to management and see if I can get her a temporary spot in the Green Zone." Knowing my case was best made in person, I rushed over to the Republican Palace where the Management Offices were located. Even though it was Sunday, I figured a few Americans were bound to be in the office. In Embassy Baghdad, the concept of "weekends" didn't exist, people worked at least six, if not seven, days a week. "Weekend" just meant you could sleep in a little before heading to work.

Darting from desk to desk, I was finally referred to an individual in charge of housing assignments who was also in a senior enough position to deal with exceptional situations. But he wasn't in the office. Refusing to be deterred, I got on the phone again and interrupted his weekend afternoon. Rushing over my words, I was close to panicking, desperately hoping I could literally save Asha from death. I pleaded with him to make an exception and temporarily permit Asha to stay in the Green Zone. Allowing local staff to live in the Green Zone was normally not done. There were far too many Iraqis to accommodate them all. And it was difficult to institute a fair policy that would allow some Iraqis to live among the Americans but not others. I begged.

Acquiescing to my request, he finally said, "I have one temporary place available. She can use it, but likely only for a couple of months."

Hurriedly, I gushed, "Thank you, thank you, thank you so much, I really owe you one for this." I hung up, anxious to call Asha back, the one hour was up.

Expecting my call, she answered on the first ring. I said, "I have some great news. You can come live in the Green Zone, but likely only for a couple of months. And you have to try and not let the other Iraqis know about this. We want to keep it as quiet as possible."

Thinking she'd be grateful, I was a little surprised when she said, "Amy, I really appreciate you finding me a place to live in the Green Zone, but I can't move there."

"Why not?" I asked incredulously, adding, "It's the only way I know to keep you safe."

"I want to, but I can't do that to my family. If the insurgents find out I'm living in the Green Zone, then they'll know I'm still working for the Americans, and they'll kill my mom and my brothers for sure. I can't come to the Green Zone. I could never live with myself if something happened to them." Then she asked, "I only have a few vacation days available. Do you think I could take some leave without pay and just stay home for a little while in case they're watching the house?"

Feeling helpless and defeated, but understanding her reaction, I said, "I don't know. Let me talk to Dick. Take a vacation day tomorrow and I'll give you a call then and let you know what I can work out."

Being short of one staff member, it was a busy day in the office the next day, but I talked Dick about Asha's request. He agreed that she could use all her vacation time and take some leave without pay, "But eventually," he said, leaving the timeline a little open, "she will either have to return to work or quit."

Calling Asha, I said, "You can use your vacation and then take some leave without pay. I'm not sure how much time we can give you though, likely not more than six to eight weeks."

Relieved by this news, Asha and I spent a few minutes chatting. I vowed to call her again the next day to check in, I hung up feeling helpless and worried about my friend. We soon fell into a routine of talking every evening after I got off work. I not only missed seeing her in the office but also wanted to make sure that she was holding up under the pressure of her insurgent-imposed house arrest. Understandably, she sounded a little down some days, as her life fell into a pattern of helping with housework and cooking. Occasionally, she would dare to peep out a curtain, but she refused to step outside, lest she put her family in danger. "I made dolmas today," she'd say despondently when I asked how her day was. However, for the most part, she appeared to be holding up rather well, given the circumstances.

Closer than ever, I treasured our chats and I know Asha did too. On more than one occasion, she said, "Amy, you are my angel. Your calls are helping me get through this." And eventually, after a couple of months, Asha had to make a decision—return to the office or quit her job at the embassy. There had been no more threats from the insurgents since that initial note, so she hoped whomever had left it was either dead or had moved on. She decided she needed the job and would take the risk and return to work. Thankfully, it seemed that the insurgents had indeed moved on, because she didn't hear from them again and we soon settled back into our work life together.

One day I asked, "How is it possible that you, the beautiful sunny person that you are, can be a product of Iraq and its many wars? If I had your life," I said, "I think the trauma would render me incapable of getting up in the morning."

Her response consisted of two simple words, "My mother." She went on to explain that she first learned about war when she was seven. Her next-door neighbor and soccer coach, whom she idolized and thought of as her "best friend," was killed on the frontlines of the Iran–Iraq War. When his mother heard the news, her horrible, gut-wrenching screams reverberated up and down Asha's street. Asha said, "I'll never forget that scream."

The Iran–Iraq War lasted eight long years, taking Asha through elementary and middle school. Living through it, she recounted, "I learned things kids shouldn't know or have to worry about. Like it's important to keep your bedroom window open a crack at all times, that way it won't shatter during a bombing raid; that nearby explosions and gunfire didn't necessarily mean immediate danger, but the wail of a war siren did. A war siren meant you had to run home immediately." The sound of explosions became part of her everyday childhood. "Background noise," she said.

Something I was starting to relate to a bit. Less than three years after the Iran–Iraq War ended, the first Gulf War started and Iraq was at war, again. Asha said, "I felt robbed. I was getting ready to graduate high school. I should have been excited about going to college and then finding a job. But we were at war. Again. And then the sanctions destroyed our economy and life for middle- and lower-class Iraqis." She added, "Many of my friends and family decided to leave." But, through it all, Asha and her family stayed in Baghdad. It was their land, their country, their home. They weren't ready to give up on it. Even in the face of years of war and the sanctions against Iraq, Asha managed to graduate from college.

After that, she was finally ready to start her life, then there were the bombing raids in 1998. Little remembered by the American public, Operation Desert Fox was a bombing campaign carried out by the United States and the United Kingdom for Iraq's failure to comply with United Nations Security Council resolutions and its interference with United Nations Special Commission inspectors.

Asha said, "The bombings only lasted for a few days, but they reminded me of what war can bring, or how close we are to war. Most of my family and friends that were still here had enough. They sold all their stuff and tried to find a way to leave, becoming refugees or asylees." However, Asha and her family continued to stay in Iraq.

"Then it was 2003 and all Iraqis knew that war was inevitable. "Yet again." said Asha, "I was done. I couldn't live through another war. I thought that either the Americans would kill me or Saddam would blow up the country rather than surrender."

Asha told her mother about her fears, saying "I can't survive another war. I can't go through the bombings. I can't see the bodies pile up. I can't stand in line for food. I can't live with limited water and electricity and the anxiety of it all. I'm done."

But her mother was having none of it, "Asha, you have to live like a survivor. None of us know what will happen next, but you can't give up and live like you're already dying. Even in the most horrific natural disasters, like earthquakes and tsunamis, there are always survivors. And that's what you are. You are a survivor, Asha."

"With those words," Asha said, "I started living life like a survivor. I decided to focus on the sunshine wherever I could find it."

Moved almost to tears by Asha's story and how the strength of her mother got her through yet another war, and Asha's own ability to seek out happiness and joy even in dire conditions, I jumped up and gave her a big hug.

I think the other Iraqi women had been listening to our conversation, as they came over and also started sharing war stories from their child-hoods. Nadira, being the comic of the group, lightened the mood and made us all laugh.

Nadira said that during the Iran–Iraq War, to show their patriotism, she and the other young Iraqi schoolchildren were encouraged to draw pictures of Iraq triumphing over the Iranian military. Then, when she was about six, her family moved to England for a short time. She attended a British school, and on one of her initial days, her teacher told the children to draw pictures. Using a red crayon to put the finishing touches on her artwork, Nadira proudly walked over and, beaming, showed her teacher her masterpiece. She was particularly pleased with herself and expected a lot of praise. Her teacher took one look, put her hand over hear heart, and looking horrified said, "I think I had better meet your parents." Nadira, as she told it, had drawn a glorious battle scene with Iraqi fighter jets and bombs and tanks killing Iranian soldiers. It was complete with images of blood-soaked Iranian bodies. Nadira laughed as she said, "After the parent-teacher conference, I quickly learned how to draw rainbows and butterflies and sunshines like all the other little girls in my class."

CHAPTER 10:

Office Space, Baghdad-Style

After my first day of meeting my colleagues and getting a crash course in war zone realities, my workday pretty quickly settled into a routine.

5:15: Roll out of bed and throw on my gym clothes.

5:20: Meet a trailer neighbor/my American Consular coworker outside her hooch (a.k.a. trailer) and make the ten- to fifteen-minute walk across the palace compound to the nice, big military gym—we were allowed to use.

5:30–5:45: Begin cardio workout followed by a little circuit training.

6:30–6:45: Finish workout and walk to the DFAC with my gym buddy for breakfast. Get two hard-boiled eggs, mayo and mustard packs, and some salt and pepper. Make my own egg salad and eat it on a piece of toast.

7:10: Finish breakfast and return to trailer to shower and get ready for work (based on my timeline, this was not a very involved process as mentioned; I'm a let-my-hair-dry-naturally person).

7:30: Walk to my car and drive the roughly two miles to my office.

8:00: After checking email, began processing passport applications or adjudicating visa requests.

12:00: Take a lunch break at the U.S. Agency for International Development (USAID) DFAC. USAID had a separate living, working compound that was relatively close to the U.S. Embassy where I worked. USAID also had a small DFAC, so it was much easier and faster to eat there instead of returning to the DFAC at the Palace for lunch.

12:30: Return to work for an afternoon of interviewing visa and passport applicants, and processing applications.

5:00 or 6:00: Finish work for the day and return to the Palace compound to enjoy dinner at the DFAC.

7:00: Depending on the day, I'd either report to a health and wellness class (Karate, Hula Dancing, or Belly Dancing), do laundry, catch a movie at the Palace movie theater, meet up with friends for poolside board games and drinks, or go to a local party or bar.

10:00: Weekday bedtime in order to make my early morning workout.

In some respects, my typical workday resembled that of any other office worker around the world. I once joked that we were living *Office Space*, Baghdad-style. The movie *Office Space* is about a bored and frustrated office worker whose reality did not meet his expectations. On a routine basis, the protagonist dealt with printer errors, report shuffling, and mundane work. That was my life for one year. I lived *Office Space*. Except that my report shuffling, notarizing, and application processing was interrupted by regular gunfire, arranging the rescue of a runaway American teenager, and the heartbreaking misery of war. My reality oscillated between the mostly mundane to the occasionally horrifying. Plenty of my days consisted of notarizing documents and processing passport applications for the military. For some reason, the Department of Defense sent our U.S. Military personnel to Baghdad without passports. I'm not sure if this was common practice, or if it had been out of necessity in an effort to quickly deploy troops. Unfortunately, soldiers couldn't take an international vacation without a passport, so as a Consular Officer, I approved many passport applications.

While processing passports for the military is done at multiple embassies and consulates around the world, *Office Space* Baghdad-style met that I once processed the passports of three American terrorists. The Americans were members of the Islamo-Marxist totalitarian cult, a former designated terrorist organization, the Mojahedin-e Khalq (MEK). They wanted to travel to the United States for medical treatment. The State Department disclosed that they would likely be met at the airport by the FBI, but they wanted to return anyway. After some back and forth with Washington DC about whether Americans who are members of a designated terrorist organizations should hold U.S. passports, Dick flew to Camp Ashraf where the terrorists were living to collect their passport applications and photos. It was logistically and bureaucratically much easier for Dick to fly to them, as opposed to figuring out how to get terrorists into the Embassy. For about one minute I was excited, thinking I'd get to leave the Green Zone and make the trip, but Dick nominated himself courier instead. When he returned and handed me their passport applications to enter into the adjudication system, for one brief moment, I felt like I was part of political history, which was in total contrast to how I normally felt.

I hated it when I walked around Saddam's old palace and soldiers would yell across the room, "Hey, it's the passport lady!" or "Hey, it's the notary lady!"

"Whoo-hoo," I'd think to myself, "I'm the passport lady." I was a bright-eyed, bushy-tailed optimist who'd joined the Foreign Service to change the world, one foreign interaction at a time, not to adjudicate passports for the military. However, the humbling, and to be honest, frankly boring nature of the job was better than my day being interrupted by other duties. A prime example of "be careful what you wish for."

One day, someone from the State Department's Hostage Rescue Team came to the Consular section with a suitcase, which Dick directed them to put in my office cubicle. Not sure what was going on, I asked Dick, "What's going on? Whose suitcase is this?" He said it belonged to a hostage victim and that I needed to make careful notations of its contents. I wasn't really sure what I was supposed to do, processing possessions of hostage victims fortunately was not a common occurrence and therefore not something I felt properly trained to do. I don't remember it being covered in my DC Consular training course. I ended up taking a common-sense approach and decided if I made careful notations, my work could not be faulted. Pulling out a yellow steno pad and pen, I got down on the carpeted floor next to my chair and sitting cross-legged, I unzipped the suitcase right there in the middle of my cubicle where it had been delivered. I slowly rifled through the contents, taking copious notes. The items were typical of what you'd expect, socks, underwear, a couple of t-shirts with the military color scheme.

The whole process was unbelievably surreal. I can't really explain the feeling. First, words cannot adequately describe how sad and awful it is to handle the effects of someone who is being held hostage *at that very moment*. I wondered what he was going through on a daily basis, was he being tortured or left alone. Was he being fed adequate food or were they starving him? Was he was allowed to use the bathroom or shower, or did he just had to wallow in his excrement? Inevitably, my mind then wandered to how I would cope in a similar situation. How would I occupy my time, if I wasn't being tortured and beaten unconscious? Would the terrorists rape me? Or would some religious code prevent them from doing so? Would I get really good at push-ups? Or would I take a dream vacation in my head? Going to Baghdad, we were all told the price that would be on our heads if we were kidnapped. Small-time or local kidnappers sometimes sell hostages to more notorious criminals, who have a bigger stage to exploit the crime. At the time, I think American women were more valuable than American men. So, I was fully cognizant of the price on my own head. I don't remember exactly what that was, if I had to guess I'd say it was about $150,000–$200,000.

After going down the mind rabbit-hole of wondering what it would be like to be a hostage victim, I snapped myself out of my reverie and reminded myself that cataloging the contents of the suitcase wasn't about me. At that particular point in time, my life was actually about a horribly unfortunate American. But if I put a stop to thinking about me, then I had to actually focus on what I was doing. It felt voyeuristic looking through someone's private belongings. Thinking about it still gives me a bad taste in my mouth. There is no training that can prepare you for that kind of stuff. Whenever the news reports that an American in another country has been kidnapped, there's most likely a Consular Office cataloging and documenting their personal possessions that were left behind.

That suitcase sat in my cubicle for months, a silent, daily reminder of one man's tragedy in a warzone. I remember the day that the Hostage Team returned to the office asking for the suitcase back. Initially anxious about their request, they quickly assured me the news was good. The hostage was released and was returning home. Smiling, like I hadn't done in months, I handed it over.

CHAPTER 11:

Marla Ruzicka

Going through a hostage victim's belongings fortunately was not a common occurrence. At least six Americans were kidnapped while I was in Iraq, but I only ever cataloged the belongings of one. A horribly depressing, but common, task I often did do was track down information on deceased American civilians and create their death certificates. Typically, the deceased were Department of Defense contractors. And sometimes the contracting companies didn't bother to notify the Consular Section that an American had died. We'd learn about it in the newspaper, along with the rest of the country. I'd then have to find the appropriate corporate personnel and get the necessary information to get the death certificate paperwork started.

On occasion, other governments contacted our section to help locate information on their deceased civilians as well. I remember one tricky case where my British counterpart reached out to me because the body of a deceased UK citizen, who worked for an American contracting company, was being stored in a freezer by the Korean Military in northern Iraq. The Brits were having a difficult time tracking down the deceased man and transporting his body home.

I lost count of how many death certificates I signed after I hit 160. The first was hard. Actually, they were all hard. But, for me, the worst one was signing Marla Ruzicka's death certificate. I believe she was the only nonmilitary contractor whose death certificate I processed.

Marla lived the life I could have chosen, but I had lacked the courage. We were about the same age and although I don't know this for sure, I like to imagine we shared some similar interests. But back in late 2001, when I was presented with two opportunities—one was to work with the United Nations High Commission for Refugees in Afghanistan, and the other to become a diplomat with the U.S. State Department. I weighed my options: dig latrines in a refugee camp in Afghanistan or become a diplomat—the decision seemed very easy and obvious to me—become a diplomat. Marla chose differently—she chose to go Afghanistan and confront the horrors of war.

From Afghanistan, Marla went on to Iraq. She was a powerhouse. Forming the Campaign for Innocent Victims in Conflict (later the name was changed to the Center for Civilians in Conflict)—Marla took on the entire U.S. Government and worked to convince policy makers that we had a moral obligation and duty to compensate Iraqi civilians and their families who were killed or injured by United States Military efforts. Armed with the results of a survey she conducted by literally knocking on doors in war-torn Iraq, Marla went to Washington. She got the attention of Senator Patrick Leahy (D-Vermont), who sponsored legislation to provide U.S. aid to Iraqi civilians that had been harmed by the U.S. Military. But Marla didn't stop there, she continued fighting for more—until April 16, 2005. That day, a car bomber likely aiming for a U.S. Military entourage, went for the softer target instead and took out the car Marla and her translator were traveling in. According to media reports, she'd been on her way to help one more family before going to a party she had organized at her hotel. Marla was twenty-eight.

Marla was killed several months before I arrived in Iraq. But within days, my Iraqi coworkers told me all about her. She had been to the embassy shortly before her death to add new visa pages to her passport. They said her smile lit up the waiting room and that she had a kind word for everyone she met. The Iraqis discussed Marla like she was a celebrity—she was larger than life in their eyes, a real hero. She was the only American civilian they knew who put her life at risk to navigating the country, unprotected, to fight for them and their rights.

After telling me how absolutely amazing Marla was, Nadira said she had something to show me. Mildly curious, I couldn't interpret her look—if it was something good or bad, so I followed her across the office to a couple of metal filing cabinets. She opened one of the drawers and pulled out two glossy 8 × 10 photos, that had been taken at the scene of Marla's car bombing—and, almost proudly, held them up for me to see. I'm not sure why she felt compelled to share the images with me—they were pictures of the bombed-out car and a burned body. I felt like an unwilling vulture—momentarily stunned as I gaped at the photos. Almost as if the wind had been knocked out of me. The body was burned beyond recognition, I couldn't even tell if it was Marla or her translator. I closed my eyes to shut out the horrific images, colors made more vivid by the twisted metal and burned oil and gas and bomb accelerants. To this day, I can still see those photos. And when I think about Marla, I'm always overwhelmed by simultaneous feelings of shock, sadness, fear, outrage, and humility. She must have known the risks she was taking to help Iraqi civilians and yet she took them anyway. Turning away from the images my colleague was still holding, I silently walked silently back to my desk and slumped down into my chair, feeling numb and empty.

There was usually a month or longer lag between a death and issuing the formal death certificate. On the day I had to sign Marla's, I sat at my desk bawling. I was tempted to include a personal note to her parents, telling them how amazing their daughter was, how many Iraqi lives she had touched and how she would forever be an inspiration to me personally on how to live a life full of purpose and meaning. I couldn't help but think that if each human being had just a tenth of the compassion that Marla did for innocent victims of unspeakable atrocities, the world would be a much better place for us all. But I didn't write that note. I didn't know if it was appropriate or would be welcomed. So, I signed and then ever so gently placed the required ten copies of the death certificate in an envelope, sealed it, and sat back feeling immensely inadequate. I wanted to personally touch the family, but instead, I remained bound by my government bureaucratic role. Wiping away my tears, I squashed overwhelming emotions into some deep dark place, to deal with another time, and got up to interview yet another passport applicant from the frontlines somewhere that wanted to go on vacation tomorrow.

CHAPTER 12:

Welcome to the Wild West

Just as my days in the office quickly slipped into a routine, or as much as they could considering where I was, so too did my life in the Green Zone. Living in the Green Zone was a bit like living in the Wild West. Not in the horse-riding, chaps-wearing, cowboy hat sort of way—but in the gun-toting, lack of central authority, not abiding by existing social mores type of existence, basically the lawlessness part of the Wild West.

The Green Zone was a four-square mile area in Central Baghdad that had been delineated and fortified by the U.S. Military in 2003. Entry and exit from the Green Zone was controlled by armed guards. It stood in contrast to the Red Zone, or the rest of Baghdad. Nestled on the Tigris River, it was formerly the home to Saddam, his sons, and his Ba'athist loyalists. His palace was complete with palatial pools (really palatial with enormously high diving boards), expansive gardens, and wide boulevards that served as parade routes.

A picture of one of the palatial pools.

When the U.S. Military seized the area, they constructed strategic walls topped with razor wire and cordoned it off from the rest of the city. Like any section of a city, before that it contained a mix of government offices, monuments, recreational facilities, hotels, hospitals, restaurants, retail stores, clubs, apartments, and single-family homes. When it became the Green Zone, those existing facilities continued to operate, they were just augmented by U.S. Government dining facilities (DFACS), a military shopping complex (PX) complete with a Pizza Hut, multiple trailer parks to house American personnel, and a spacious gym. Many of the existing businesses and services were allowed to continue operating independently, while some vital services, like the hospital, came under U.S. command. The United States allowed members of other countries—the "Coalition of the Willing"—to headquarter within the Green Zone, while some Iraqis also managed to stay or scamper in and occupy former Ba'athist homes, before the borders were completely secured.

Side Note: The term "Coalition of the Willing" was coined by the George W. Bush Administration to describe countries that supported the U.S. invasion of Iraq and subsequent postwar efforts. I'm not sure if there's any truth to it, but I remember hearing a story that Canada had wanted to observe a coalition meeting, and as a result, the United States added its name to the list of official members. As the story goes, Canada repeatedly insisted that they were just observers, not actual members.

For those countries that had not joined our coalition, their embassies were only permitted in the Red Zone, "Sorry, France; sorry, Germany—good luck on the outside…don't let the razor wire hit you on the way out," is basically what we said.

The Green Zone was an eclectic mix of individuals. As far as Americans were concerned, the military obviously had the largest presence. But there were also civilian employees from the Departments of State (DOS), Defense (DOD), Agriculture (USDA), Commerce (DOC), Homeland Security (DHS), Health and Human Services (HHS), Justice (DOJ), Labor (DOL), Transportation (DOT), Treasury (USDT), the Agency for International Development (USAID), all of the alphabet soup folks, along with various private contractors. The majority of the Americans lived and worked in or around Saddam's Republican Palace. Some contractors were professionals, advising the Iraqi ministries as their new government got up and running; others were paid mercenaries, truck drivers, maintenance personnel, and so on, including anything and everything necessary to move people and resources through a big war zone. Confined to the Green Zone, I was fascinated by stories from people who actually left it on a daily basis. I met one contractor who was in charge of constructing cell phone towers. He said that he had rebuilt the same cell phone tower three or four times, because insurgents repeatedly blew it up. Surprisingly, he didn't appear frustrated by the repetitive nature of his job—he seemed resigned to it, sadly so.

Because the military carried loaded guns at all times, and commanders like to "maintain good order and discipline," soldiers fell under "General Order #1"—which basically stated no drinking, no sex, no porn, no gambling, or anything that might distract or impair their use of live weapons or damage their credibility with the Iraqi Government, the United States was after all, no longer at war with Iraq. The rest of us (including military contractors) did not have to abide by these rules. There was drinking, a lot of drinking, a lot of parties, and a lot of bars back in 2005 and 2006.

The State Department's Regional Security Office and many of the various military contracting companies set up bars in the Green Zone that were open to the public, primarily on weekends. It's unclear whether they were legally allowed to establish these watering holes in the Green Zone, but they did it anyway. I frequented establishments like, "Lock 'n Load" and "The Bunker Bar." There was also the Baghdad Country Club, that I recall (I believe several different establishments used this name over the years) didn't focus on serving drinks to foreigners like the Western bars. Its customers were primarily Iraqi. There was lots of dancing and amazing local food. There was one time when I got caught up in a Dabkah, a regional folk dance where men and women join hands and dance in a circle. As the Arabic music blared, those of us dancing progressively moved faster, until the walls beyond the smiling faces of the dancers blurred, and we practically collapsed, out of breath.

Many of the military contractors I met were creepy assholes, more about this later. But my friends and I went to their Western bars anyway because there really wasn't much else going on in the Green Zone and alcohol was a good escape. My friends primarily consisted of Joe and his coworkers. We frequented the bars together, so there was usually a posse to protect me from other men. I can only recall one time when we were at a contracting company party bar that my spidey sense started tingling when I was accidently separated from Joe. We were at a house owned by the Olive Group, and there were too many drunken people, crammed into too small of a space, with too many groping hands and wandering eyes. I desperately found my friends again and suggested that we leave before the party got out of hand.

My preferred place to blow off steam though was at foreign embassy parties. Unfortunately, they tended to be by *Invite Only*, and it wasn't always easy to secure an invitation. People rotated in and out of Baghdad constantly, so by the time we met and established a friendship with a non-American, chances were they were on their way out the door—and so too were our chances of getting our names on a list. Receiving an invite to the Italian compound was seen as a golden ticket, it felt like winning the lottery. I'd heard about the Italian parties for *months* before I was finally invited. The Italian Embassy's compound had a real brick oven in the backyard—in a war zone. Walking through the doors to the outdoor grounds was like entering a beautiful oasis. Most of Baghdad was dusty and dirty, and everything in the Green Zone had that military tan look topped with sandbags and razor wire. However, the Italian compound was different; it was lush and green, and even the air seemed cleaner, or maybe that was our imagination. There were lemon trees and red-and-white striped awnings, with a patio surrounding the outdoor pizza oven. The Italians made fresh pizza for their party guests but never enough to go around, as soon as a pie was pulled out of the oven, it was completely devoured. I only managed to get one slice, but it was heavenly, warm in my hands, smelled delicious, and I was filled with anticipation as I took my first bite.

The Brits were a fun lot, too. Their compound had a great setup with a bar, a pool, and a dance floor. The British were quirky though about what side of the street you had to drive on to get to their embassy. American-style driving dominated the rest of the Green Zone—we drove on the right side of the road. But when approaching the British Embassy, on the little stretch of road that the Brits controlled, approaching cars had to switch lanes and drive on the left side.

The most exclusive parties, of course, were held by the CIA. They had their own separate compound, isolated from the rest of us U.S. Government employees. And they didn't let just anyone through their gates. A codeword was required to get into their parties, which changed each time. Their parties weren't very fun though, it was more the thrill of being allowed to enter the nest of spies. A lot of the CIA people didn't mingle with us nonspies at these parties. They'd just stand around and send furtive glances our way all night, eyeing (and probably summing us up) over their gin and tonics.

At one of these CIA events, I was walking from the bar to an outdoor table our group had claimed, and practically ran into a CIA guy that I recognized from a previous tour. I quickly held my drink aloft trying to avoid spilling it down the front of my tee-shirt. We weren't really friends, more like acquaintances. Not sure if he knew it, but my State Department colleagues and I had nicknamed him and his wife *Ken and Barbie*, because they were both beautiful and smiley and shiny and perfect. Not that I was intimidated by their good looks and sexy spy allure, well maybe a little, but nonetheless, I managed to ask him what I thought was a simple question, "How do you like working in Baghdad?" I'll never forget his response as it was not what I expected, I'd thought we were just doing the small-talk thing.

Instead, he launched right in, "It's awesome. In most countries we have to ask permission of the host government before we take out the bad guys—here we just kill them."

Unsure how to respond to his matter-of-fact almost gleeful killing of other human beings, even if they were the bad guys, my wheels were turning slowly by that point in the evening, I simply raised my eyebrows at him, thinking, "Great..."

Wanting to shut down the conversation before he divulged any other nuggets, I threw out an, "Awesome, well, I'll see you around," and then I turned and finished wobbling back to my friends.

Despite my description, free time in the Green Zone wasn't all just parties and bars. And the partying wasn't the only thing though that made it feel like the lawless Wild West. It was more this sense that the men—somehow felt that they were above the law—or at least emboldened to act inappropriately. (I say men because the non-Iraqis in the Green Zone were predominantly that, men). My friend once described the Green Zone culture of the time as one of "swinging dicks." Her description seemed pretty appropriate.

The most brazen men of them all were the contractors that provided security services. I apologize to security services personnel who are actually good guys; I know it only takes a few bad apples to spoil the bunch. I can also fully appreciate that it takes a special reckless sort-of daredevil to consistently gear up for high-speed car runs, ferrying diplomats and other officials to meetings with Iraqis through some pretty dangerous neighborhoods. There's a certain confidence, swagger, and attitude that seems to accompany that type of profession. Following societal norms and basic human principles can become a casualty to those teetering daily on the edge of life and death. They were brash with their words and obtrusive with their actions.

As part of the military's health and wellness campaign, Department of Defense employees with particular skills or expertise were encouraged to teach evening classes, in an effort to keep the rest of us busy, occupied, happy, and social. I'm a joiner and always game for trying something new, so I signed up for every class that fit my schedule and interest. I took karate, hula dancing, and belly dancing. Karate was my favorite—at least learning the moves and doing kata. I never actually wanted to fight anyone, or, let's be honest, take a roundhouse to the face. Our instructor was a really nice reservist who was a black belt in karate and a police officer in the states.

The hula and belly dancing classes were fun, mostly because it was an opportunity for women to get together as a community and support each other, as women were few and far between in the Green Zone.

For two straight hours (the classes were back-to-back) twice a week, half-a-dozen of us danced and talked and laughed and didn't see a single man the entire time. It was heavenly. And frankly, it felt like a mini-vacation from being ogled or propositioned even while donning my belly-dancing bra top and jangly hip scarf. In addition to being an accomplished member of the armed forces and dancer, our instructor was a seamstress who made costumes for us, for free. We just had to provide a strapless bra for her to sew under the colorful, bedecked top.

Our teacher once asked if we would be game to perform on stage for the troops at an upcoming event in the Green Zone. Most of the other belly dancers were up for it—but another woman and I vehemently objected. First, let's be honest, I still sucked and don't like doing anything halfway, I'm too competitive for that. And second, and more importantly, there was absolutely no way I was going to belly dance in front of potentially thousands of sex-starved men, that hadn't seen a woman's body in six months or even longer. That just sounded like a horrible idea and I wasn't willing to subject myself to the objectification that would have inevitably followed. As we discussed the possibility, someone suggested that we could hide our identities by veiling our faces. My response was, "No fucking way am I doing that. Hiding our identities would just further objectify us." I then thought, but didn't say, "If you want to get raped as you make your way off-stage, go ahead."

Our instructor apparently didn't have the same qualms about gyrating with abdomen and cleavage exposed in front of others. On one occasion she agreed to be the entertainment at a small, exclusive, rooftop going away party. There were maybe a maximum of thirty people invited. She needed help with her props (finger symbols), queuing her music, and so on—so she asked me if I could assist. After triple-checking that I would not be asked to dance with her, I acquiesced. In fact, I kind of got into it, thinking it might be a fun party.

And while completely out-of-character for me, I thought it might even be nice to feel feminine at the party—so I decided to paint my toenails pink—

sounds innocuous enough. What's the big deal about pink toenails? Well, for me, it was kind of a big deal at the time. I had been living in a war zone for at least six months, maybe more by then, surrounded predominantly by men. I was tired of the daily catcalls as I walked around the Green Zone. I was tired of the constant stares, being an oddity as a youngish woman. I was tired of trying to remember not to smile at strangers, because a smile was seen as an invitation to talk, or more.

Obviously, I didn't like being noticed in Baghdad. Encounters when looks or remarks on my being a girl, sadly left me feeling gross and dirty. It's amazing how demeaning a look could feel.

At the six-month point, painting my toenails, was myself acknowledging for the first time, in a long time, that I was a woman. I left my trailer for the party that night with an extra skip in my step. I arrived on time, and everything was proceeding according to plan. I handed off the finger symbols when needed and queued the music correctly. The crowd was engaged, but not being gross. I relaxed. My job almost done, I leaned against the wall, enjoying the night air and the breeze sweeping across the rooftop party and watching my friend finish her performance. My harassment-vigilance guard was down. It was then that a stranger approached me, a military contractor—he was a big dude too—tall, quite full around the middle. He leaned against the wall next to me, lowered his lips down to my ear I guess to be heard above the music and said in a southern drawl, "Those are about the prettiest little toes I've ever seen."

Not really wanting to engage, but compelled by basic human nature to respond, I simply said, "Thanks." Mistakenly thinking we could just leave it at that.

Apparently, my simple response was an invitation for more conversation if you can call it that. Foregoing any further small talk, he then just came out and said, "I'll give you fifty bucks if you sleep with me."

I'm one of those people who always thinks of a million amazing things to say ten minutes too late. So, I didn't really respond. I just gaped at his audacity, gave him a disgusted look, and walked away. I was fuming, I was livid. I was thinking, "Who does he think he is to approach me like that? Is that how he was taught to talk to women? In what world is it OK to just ask a random woman to sleep with you for money? How would he feel if someone did that to his mother or sister? Does he not see how disrespectful he is being? And furthermore, who does he think *I am*? I am a diplomat for God's sake. I'm not some cheap prostitute." I was horrified—and, besides that, I'm definitely worth more than fifty bucks! That's when I really felt like I was living in a lawless Wild West. I haven't painted my toenails since.

Travelers Guide to the Green Zone

I sometimes joked with my friends in Baghdad that we should write our own traveler's guide to the Green Zone, complete with restaurant reviews, sites of interest, and shopping tips for future diplomats. For the adventurer, or bored, there was plenty to keep one occupied. My friends and I never got around to writing it, but here it is: *The 2005 Official Travelers Guide to the Green Zone.*

Fine Dining Establishments:

DFAC (short for dining facility): This was the main eating establishment in the Green Zone. It was free. It was big. It operated buffet style. There were barrels and sandbags outside the doors, reminding gun-toting individuals to clear their weapons prior to entry. It provided all the basic American comfort food. Once, the chefs tried to do something special for Thanksgiving or Christmas and served shrimp. Thank goodness I'm a vegetarian, because everyone who ate the shrimp got food poisoning that year. I suspect somewhere between the boat and the city; it wasn't properly refrigerated.

U.S. Agency for International Development (USAID) DFAC: On the other side of the Green Zone from the main DFAC was the USAID compound, complete with its own mini-cafeteria. It was also free and much more intimate. The food featured more local flavors compared to the massive DFAC. It was there that I first fell in love with okra in tomato sauce—although the vegetables probably weren't always washed well. I fell ill with stomach conditions more than once in Baghdad after eating lunch in the USAID

DFAC. One time, I was ill enough to warrant a fluid IV. I guess even being a vegetarian didn't protect me from food-borne illnesses.

Al Rasheed DFAC: I never actually ate at the Al Rasheed Hotel DFAC, so I cannot comment on its quality or ambiance. But there was one there in 2005 and 2006 in the lobby restaurant.

Fast food: For those wanting to venture off-site, but still stay in mini-America, there were multiple fast-food options near the PX, including Pizza Hut and Subway.

Chinese: Located within the Green Zone was one Chinese restaurant. If you didn't know where it was, it was easy to miss the narrow passageway leading back to it. Spray-painted looking graffiti of "Best Foob" with an arrow pointed the way. It was rumored that there was a massage parlor above the restaurant that provided happy endings, although no one I personally knew ever tested the rumor.

Blue Star Cafe: Not surprisingly, this restaurant catered to Westerners in the Green Zone but served Middle Eastern food. It also had the added benefit of serving beer and wine. On a nice evening, patrons could sit at the outdoor plastic tables near the palm trees decorated with Christmas lights, munching on hummus and sipping alcoholic beverages.

Shawarma stands: Alternatively, for the very adventurous, there were some amazing shawarma and falafel stands in the middle of the Iraqi areas of the Green Zone. I ventured to them only once with Joe. Appearing out of place, we were met with some questioning glances, but the food was amazing.

Green Zone Pizza Hut and entrance to Chinese restaurant,
which had the "Best Foob."

For Your Shopping Pleasure:

The PX: A staple of military bases, the Baghdad PX carried various American drinks and snacks, as well as basic clothing, toiletries, electronics, and more. A tailor and a couple of overly priced tourist shops, including a rug shop were attached to the PX. It was located across the parking lot from the Republican Palace.

Little Venice Rug Merchant: There was an area of the Green Zone nicknamed "Little Venice," likely due to its numerous cement bridges, waterways, and fountains. Those in the know never shopped at the rug store connected to the PX—instead they would trek down to the Little Venice Rug Merchant. On most days, he would park his car somewhere along the idyllic Little Venice streets, pop his truck, and spread a few rugs out on the street for tourists to buy. Full disclosure, I'm a recovering rugaholic. The Middle East does that to many folks. I may have bought a carpet or two from this fine establishment.

Al Rasheed Hotel: Located within the Al Rasheed Hotel was a tourist shop or two. That was where I purchased a couple of gimmicky lighters and watches with Saddam's face on them for friends and family. The Iraqis that I met were not fans of Saddam, but they did long for life under his rule. As one of my coworkers said to me once, "Sure, under Saddam sometimes people would disappear on their way to work, and you never heard from them again. But, for the most part, life was much better. We got along with our neighbors, our markets were full, we could go to weddings, and have parties. Now our power goes on and off, our market shelves are empty, and extremist outsiders are killing internet café owners and sellers of ice on the street corner, because 'Mohammed didn't have the Internet and in Mohammad's time there wasn't ice.'"

Counterfeit stands: Along various backstreets and alleyways, were merchants selling cheap plastic junk and counterfeit music and movies. Of course, I fully respect copyright and trademark laws and never took part in purchasing such goods. (My husband is an attorney; I feel compelled to say this, but it is really true).

Outdoor Rug Merchant in Little Venice.

Sightseeing Excursions:

Victory Arch: A popular place for taking photographs (I did pose on top of a military vehicle). Victory Arch, officially known as the Swords of Qādisīyah, consisted of statues of huge hands holding crossed swords. The two arches marked the entrances to the parade grounds constructed by Saddam Hussein to commemorate the Iran–Iraq War. Military parades are popular with dictators.

Walk of Broken Statues: The world watched the televised event of U.S. soldiers removing Saddam's statue from atop the Monument to the Unknown Soldier after the second Gulf War. And his statue wasn't the only one toppled. Scattered across the Green Zone were various piles of toppled statues.

Blown-up buildings and palaces: Scattered around the Green Zone were various blown-up structures from the war that no one had bothered to clean up or demolish yet. Sometimes, when we were bored, my friends and I would explore these places, kind of like spelunking. It probably wasn't the best of decisions from a structural safety standpoint. But there was a really cool one nearby that had an underground bunker where Saddam had reportedly hidden during the first Gulf War.

The Courthouse: Saddam's trial took place while I was in Baghdad. I happened to know some of the embassy folks who were in charge of wrangling journalists who were covering the trial—so we had a backstage pass into the place when it wasn't being used. In what was definitely not a diplomatic move, we toured the courtroom where his trial took place.

I am posing with a soldier and a flag at the Victory Arches.

Bombed-out palaces and secret underground bunkers.

The courthouse where Saddam's trial took place.

Entertainment:

Gym: The Green Zone had a huge gym. Many people left Iraq in much better shape than they arrived, simply because there wasn't much to do and going to the gym was a good way to spend time. Typical to most American gyms, it contained rows of cardio machines, free weights, and various weight machines. I tried to go as often as possible with one of my coworkers. I'll never forget her saying that she went just so she could continue to eat a bowl of ice cream every day.

Movie Theater: The lower floor of the Republican Palace contained a movie theater. It wasn't a huge theater, but could accommodate roughly fifty people. The military would often screen movies to give us something to do.

Clubs, Activities: As part of its military wellness campaign, the Department of Defense helped coordinate various classes offered by its members for those stationed in the Green Zone. This was where I took classes in karate, hula dancing, and belly dancing—but I know there were others.

Liberty Pool: The pool at the main palace was called Liberty Pool. It had several high-diving boards and was open year-round for those inclined to use it. Again, I felt bad for military women. Since the military had to carry their guns at all times, it was something of a tourist attraction to watch military women in bikinis lug around their weapons. I'm disappointed to say that even my boyfriend at the time snapped a few pictures of the sight. I felt objectified on their behalf.

Other Pool: Saddam's Palace wasn't the only one in the Green Zone with a pool. There was also the former home of his son (either Qusay or Uday[1]). If I was going to swim, this is where I went as it was closer to the embassy where I worked.

---

[1] Saddam's sons were said to be even more horrible and ruthless than their father. If you want to learn more, check this History.com article: https://www.history.com/this-day-in-history/qusay-and-uday-hussein-killed

Night Life:

After I left Iraq, I think the number of unlicensed drinking establishments was reigned in, but while I was there, there was no shortage of bars and parties. All of the major contracting companies had a bar. Various embassy compounds would host parties (most notably the British and Italians). The U.S. Embassy's Regional Security Office ran a weekend bar. There were private house parties. The list goes on. Here is a list of the places I visited relatively routinely:

- Lock 'n Load Bar

- The Bunker Bar

- The Olive House

- Baghdad Country Club

- OGA Bar

- FBI Bar

- Italian Compound

- British Compound

- Private house parties

Not my finest moment, a drunken night inside The Bunker Bar.

The U.S. Military of course was not allowed to frequent any of these alcohol-abundant establishments. I qualify for the United States because other countries had different philosophies. For example, the UK let its soldiers have one or two beers per day, which seemed reasonable. It's not like the U.S. Military didn't find ways to smuggle alcohol into their barracks. Self-medication was definitely a popular means of making it through a warzone posting. I don't think I'm saying anything shocking here.

CHAPTER 13:

Missing Pallets of Cash

Stagecoach robberies and bank heists are at the top of my Wild West stereotypes list. Robberies were happening in Baghdad, too. But the outlaws didn't need to overpower anyone, they only had to load pallets of cash off the backs of U.S. Military cargo planes or pickup trucks.

Dick and I had a discussion one day about rumors that were circulating among U.S. Government employees, of millions of missing reconstruction dollars. I'd heard something, from one of my military contacts, and wanted to verify if it was true. The extent of our conversation was me asking, "I was talking to Colonel so and so the other day and is it true that bags of reconstruction dollars have gone missing, right off the backs of C-130s?!" And he responded, whispering conspiratorially, *"I've heard…*absent functioning international monetary systems, the military was forced to fly in cash to pay for the government's post-war efforts. A lack of accountability and oversight in the chaos may have resulted in some missing dollars, but the extent and nature is not yet understood." After decades in the Foreign Service, diplomats forget how to gossip properly, they just speak in talking points. Completely unsatisfied with this watercooler chat, but believing there was likely some truth to the rumors, I left it at that.

About six months after I left Baghdad, as I sat in my office in Dubai perusing online news headlines, an article from *The Guardian* jumped out, "How the US Sent $12bn in Cash to Iraq. And Watched It Vanish." Clicking on the headline with almost heady anticipation, I read that a California congressman, through the House Oversight Committee, had started an investigation because the United States had flown almost $12 billion in shrink-wrapped $100 bills into Iraq, and millions were either missing or practically thrown away. One shipment alone of $100 bills, totally $2.4 billion, yes "billion" was flown in on June 22, 2004—just six days before the U.S. Military handed control of Iraq back to the Iraqis.

"Holy shit," I thought, sitting back and crossing my arms with satisfaction, "the rumors were totally true. $100 bills just disappeared. *I knew it. I knew it.*" What made the scandal even more remarkable was that usually "government" is synonymous with "bureaucracy." The paperwork and signatures necessary to authorize even small purchases in nonwar zones can feel excessive. But, digging further, I found a memo prepared for the House of Representatives that said one contractor received a $2 million payment stuffed in a duffel bag in shrink-wrapped bundles. And apparently, auditors discovered that a key to one of the vaults was kept in an unsecured backpack. That wasn't even the worst of it. Auditors also found that $774,300 in cash had been stolen from one division's vault. Cash payments were made from the back of a pickup truck, and cash was stored in unguarded sacks in Iraqi ministry offices. One official was given $6.75 million in cash and was ordered to spend it in one week before the interim Iraqi Government took control of Iraqi funds. The minutes from the May 2004 Coalition Provisional Authority meeting listed a $500 million security funding disbursement as "TBD." A single disbursement of half-a-billion in taxpayer dollars was *to be determined.*

While I usually try to limit my armchair quarterbacking, it's hard not to judge the sheer lack of oversight on this one. Millions of American taxpayer dollars simply vanished in Iraq. Clicking on the next headline of the day, I thought, "I hope someone is being held accountable for this gross misuse of taxpayer dollars."

I also wondered how much other, little abuses that weren't being reported on, would add up to and if anyone was looking into them?

I had first-hand knowledge of small oversights. As with any large company or government agency, U.S. operations in Baghdad had their share of waste and abuse. When I arrived in Baghdad, I was given a cell phone that was configured so my family and friends could call me just as if they were dialing a number in the U.S. and vice versa. This was pre-ubiquitous VCIP technology and pre-WhatsApp. I don't know how it worked, but I wasn't the only one issued such a phone. Every single American and Iraqi staff member seemed to have one. And when I arrived in 2005, people had been racking up massive phone bills unchecked for more than two years.

Dick called me into his office one day and handed me a piece of paper. It was an accounting of monthly phone charges attributable to the personnel in our office. It didn't list individual calls, just totals per phone line. Since I was the direct supervisor of the Iraqi staff in our office, he said, "You need to have a conversation with the staff about their cell phone usage, in particular this one," and he pointed to a monthly charge of over $1,000. "Her monthly phone bill is routinely this high or higher, which seems excessive." In her one-year of employment with the State Department, this one individual had cost American taxpayers over $12,000 in phone charges, and she was just one person. I'm not even sure how many thousands of Americans and Iraqis had U.S. Government-issued cell phones.

Approaching her, I said, "Hey, there's something I need to talk to you about…your cell phone usage has gotten a little out of control. The bill for your phone alone was over $1,000 last month. If you continue to have such large charges, we're going to have to take it away."

She stared back at me, incredulously, and said, "Sorry, no one ever told me I needed to limit my phone use. I didn't know." To her, the phone was a perk for working with the Americans, and the associated danger. I don't even know who she was calling and how much time she spent on the phone, the information I had didn't go into that level of detail. Who knows, maybe her whole neighborhood had been using it.

But that was it—that was the extent of our conversation. I don't recall any department meetings or slaps on the wrist or frankly any naming or shaming. It always made me wonder what additional overinflated spending was ignored, because we were in a war zone.

CHAPTER 14:

Oh Shit

There was the lack of social mores, the robbing of American taxpayer money, and of course, the gunfire. To continue a hopefully not too tired metaphor, another reason the Green Zone was like living in the Wild West, was the steady, constant sound of gunfire that I surprisingly came to ignore within a matter of weeks.

The same graduate school friend who encouraged me to take the Foreign Service Exam in the first place had gone to Iraq before me. We briefly overlapped in Bahrain, he as a Public Affairs Officer and I was an Economics Officer. One night after work, we sat in his office and had a long talk about life in a warzone. After sharing a couple of his more harrowing war stories, he said, "You know what's strange, Ames, it's kind of scary at first to hear constant gunfire, but after a couple of weeks, it becomes background noise. I stopped paying attention to it." He claimed this would be the case for me too, but I didn't believe him. I thought it was impossible to get to a point where I could dismiss a steady stream of gunfire as "background noise," like ignoring city traffic sounds or the foghorns in San Francisco.

He was right though. In relatively short order, I went from being shocked at seeing almost every American carrying guns (military personnel always had guns, and they were the majority) and hearing a near-constant barrage of gunfire from beyond the Green Zone walls, to dismissing it as normal. Even the oddity of seeing poolside women in bikinis with big guns slung over their shoulders became the norm.

Side note: I think pictures of military women in bikinis with their guns were most likely fodder for unofficial Green Zone pinups. Whenever I saw men (military and civilian alike) try to surreptitiously take pictures of these women, I felt horrible. They were objectified even when just trying to relax for a while.

In addition, periodically, missiles were shot into the Green Zone. They were not targeted missiles. Insurgents would just get as close as possible to the Green Zone, shoot a missile over the wall, and hope for the best as they hastily drove off. Early in my tour, I was getting ready for work when I heard the telltale whistle of an incoming missile. I panicked, my heart rate skyrocketed, and I thought, "Oh shit, oh shit, oh shit, this is it!" Frantically throwing on my PPE (helmet and flak jacket), but not bothering to clip it, I wriggled under my bed, struggling as the jacket caught on the bed frame. With my legs still kicking, exposed beyond the bed frame, the missile hit the other side of the Green Zone. I survived. Feeling a bit sheepish, I crawled out, took a couple of deep breaths, and finished getting ready for work.

Before too long, I learned to recognize how close the missile was depending on the sound of the accompanying whistle. It got to a point where one time when I was in the shower, I heard a missile coming in, and stopped shampooing my hair long enough to stick my head out from the water stream to listen and decide if I needed to take cover. After a second or two, I deduced the missile wasn't going to land close enough to worry about, so I continued with my shower. On one occasion, a missile did land really close to my trailer, close enough to do damage when I was home. But as fate would have it, it hit the tank of a nearby water truck, severely impairing its destruction.

One of my colleagues had a bad scare once. He was sick as a dog, in bed, unable to move. But he worked directly for the Ambassador, and there was something he really needed to do. Reluctantly, he sat up and dragged himself out of bed, barely making it to the office. He finished the task as quickly as possible so he could hurry home, crawl into bed, and go back to sleep. He arrived home, only to find that during the time he was at work, a missile had crashed through his trailer ceiling and landed on his bed. It was a dud and hadn't exploded, but if he'd been in that bed, he would have been dead regardless. He said he learned a lesson that day, "I'll always listen to the Ambassador and do whatever he wants—no matter what."

I had two close brushes with gunfire and death. One day, while driving back to my trailer from the office, I entered a checkpoint chute. The Marines had set up cones to force cars through a checkpoint to verify IDs, before letting vehicles pass through to the Republican Palace, where most Americans lived and worked. There were a couple of cars ahead of me in line, so when I dropped my cell phone, I figured I had a second to reach under the dashboard and grab it. My car was a manual so I wanted to get it before it interfered with my clutch. As I lifted my head up from under the dash, phone triumphantly clutched in my hand, I saw two marines aggressively advancing toward my car—one on each side. Their guns were pointed directly at my engine block. Shocked, an enormous spike of adrenaline went through me, and I dropped my phone again. I sat straight up, hands in the air, my heart palpitating about a million miles a minute. The Marine on the driver's side apparently recognized me from my repeated entries and exits at the checkpoint where he was stationed. Approaching my open window, he lowered his gun and asked, not that nicely I might add, "What were you doing under your dashboard?"

"Aah…I dropped my phone," I replied, contritely.

"Next time," he said, "just leave it until you get through the checkpoint. You're lucky we didn't shoot up your car." He added by way of explanation, "A driverless vehicle in a checkpoint can be a sign of a car bomb."

"Whoops, sorry," I flashed a sheepish smile, "I won't do it again," I added with a lilt in my voice. Struggling to get my breathing back under control and my car in gear, I drove off wondering why the whole getting your car shot up thing had not been mentioned in the weeklong war zone school. "Probably because they thought we wouldn't be doing any driving," I reminded myself.

My dropped cell phone soon became my second-closest brush with death in Baghdad. During my one year there, I left the Green Zone three times, twice for vacation and once for a quick, regional weekend getaway. Each trip meant making the harrowing jaunt to and from the Baghdad airport. One of those times, on my way back to the Green Zone, I was "lucky" enough to catch a ride on a helicopter, instead of waiting for the Rhino to come later in the evening. Such slots were coveted as open seats were usually snatched up by more important people. The helicopter I road in did not have doors. They had been removed so gunners could sit on either side, with their large, rotating guns. Taking the last open seat with a huge smile, relieved that I didn't have to sit around the dry, dusty airport for twelve to eighteen hours waiting for the Rhino, I buckled in and sat back contentedly.

Unfortunately, it just so happened that on that particular day, at that particular time, there were folks on rooftops just waiting to shoot at an American military helicopter, which they did. The next thing I knew the gunners were returning fire, and the pilot was flying these crazy maneuvers where the helicopter turns practically up on one side and then the other. Buckled in tightly with my flak jacket and helmet on, I was too shocked to think of much beyond the mantra that I repeated over and over again in my head, "Oh shit, oh shit, oh shit, oh shit!"

After landing safely in the Green Zone, the military crew acted like it was just another day in Baghdad, as they went about their post-flight landing routine—which to them, it probably was. While me, in dramatic Hollywood fashion, stumbled out of the helicopter and fell down on my knees, practically kissing the blacktop. That was my first, last, and only helo ride in the year I was in Baghdad. But, at the time, if offered another opportunity to take a helo instead of waiting for a Rhino, I would have done it in a heartbeat. Not to sound fatalistic, but when living in a war zone, it's easy to get to a place of thinking, "If it's my time to go, it's my time to go. There's not much that can be done about it. But *inshallah*, I'll be OK."

When I first moved to the Middle East, it used to drive me absolutely batty when people responded with "inshallah" for *everything*. Inshallah means "If God wills it." So, for example, when I'd try to set up a meeting for 3 p.m. on a Tuesday, I'd say, "Tuesday at 3 p.m. works for you?" And I would get back a simple, "inshallah." Silently I'd scream back at them in my head, "No, not inshallah, not inshallah, can you make it or not?"

Of course, I never said that out loud, but I didn't initially grasp the meaning of inshallah when I first heard it in Tunisia. One of the Tunisian men who reported to me used it all the time, whenever I talked to him about his tasks and deadlines. It was a bit infuriating. Until moving to the Middle East, I operated in a world where people had freewill that they chose to exercise, or not. And leaving it up to God's will to determine if something was done was a difficult concept to understand. However, after moving to Baghdad, I totally got it. While I would like to uphold every commitment, to every person I make a commitment to, sometimes unseen forces beyond my control can interrupt the best of intentions, like being delayed because I was busy getting shot at in a helicopter. So, *inshallah*, I will make a 3 p.m. meeting with you, if you schedule one.

CHAPTER 15:

Questionable Decision-Making

Now seems like as good of a time as any to step back and try to understand what the hell was going on in Iraq anyway in 2005 and 2006 that led to the constant barrage of gunfire and the occasional missile being lobbed across the Green Zone wall. I'm not going to address why the United States was even there in the first place as I feel like there are numerous scholars who have already debated that topic pretty completely.

Whatever was going on in the microcosm called the Green Zone—it was idyllic, lawful even, compared to the rest of the country. When I was in Baghdad, there was a vague notion of poor decision-making on the part of the United States, which quickly turned initially hopeful and thankful Iraqis against our efforts. But it wasn't until years later that I truly appreciated how close we'd come to getting it right, only to have multiple questionable decisions result in an Iraqi insurgency that bolstered groups such as ISIS and the Mahdi Army.

To be fair, I think it goes without saying that I was too low on the totem pole to be involved in any of the decisions I am about to question—so there are likely aspects that I just don't or can't know or understand. But I am not the only one that finds these decisions extremely questionable and reckless. They have been documented in numerous articles, books, and documentaries.

Questionably Decision 1 (chronologically, not in terms of impact): Limited planning and disregard of initial postwar relationship building that had been done. I watched an award-winning documentary about the aftermath of the second Gulf War titled, *No End in Sight*, while writing this book. It claimed that while we spent two years planning for the aftermath of World War II, officials had less than two months to plan for the end of the Iraq War. This was obviously partly a function of the length of the two wars. But there's more to it than that. Years after I left Baghdad, I had a conversation with a State Department colleague who was a part of the postwar planning process. This person said the State Department created volumes upon volumes of information to facilitate the transition to a post-Saddam Iraq, which they took to planning meetings with the Department of Defense. Reportedly, the Defense Department routinely ignored the work done by the State Department and repeatedly ignored the State Department calls for more bodies to get the work done. Out of frustration, my colleague said that the State Department personnel got up and walked away from the table with the Defense Department, basically saying, "At least we'll be able to say we told you so when it all goes to hell."

I often think about this story and its ramifications. Decisions made in offices in the United States can reverberate around the world in ways not fully appreciated at the time they are made or by the people who are making them. Iraqis were sentenced to death by these postwar decision makers. I wonder if they appreciated the gravity of the situation or if they just saw numbers on paper.

It also makes me think about the lack of value placed on expert advice. Rampant backlash against intellectualism is difficult for me to understand. Back in 2000, I remember thinking that George. W. Bush was the first of America's anti-intellectual presidents, who eschewed an air of down-home folksiness. I could imagine having a beer with him. But I don't want a president that I can have a beer with. I want a president who is so much smarter than me that I'm intimidated to even think about having a conversation with them. I want our best and brightest to be making the big decisions.

Finally, it drives home for me the idea that when making important decisions, we should value diversity of opinion, not ignore it. Willfully choosing to exist in an echo chamber can have dangerous outcomes, as the aftermath of the Iraq War exemplified.

Questionable Decision 2: Coalition Provisional Authority Order 1: Complete De-Baathification of Iraqi Society. Politically, Saddam Hussein Was a Baathist. Baathism was a political ideology that gained ground in both Iraq and Syria post-World War II. A secular political ideology, it embraced both Arab nationalism and socialism. In Saddam's totalitarian dictatorship of a country, in order to have a government job, one had to swear allegiance to the Baathist Party—even if in name only. In other words, there were likely a large number of highly qualified government employees who understood how to run a country, and were Baathists on paper only, because they needed a job. And what did the United States do? We fired them all, rendering the most knowledgeable technocrats, who had experience running a country, unemployed. Such decisions not only were unpopular with the people but also tended to make governing more difficult, as no one with any experience was left to govern.

Questionable Decision 3: Coalition Provisional Authority Order Number 2: Dissolution of the Iraqi Military, Security, and Intelligence Infrastructure. With one swoop of a pen, the United States dissolved the Iraqi military and security services, putting 500,000 highly trained and armed military men on the streets of Iraq. These weren't pencil pushers like the Baathist technocrats; they were trained and armed soldiers. Many of whom were proud heads of household, sole breadwinners, and patriots. They wanted a stable Iraq more than the United States did. They could have helped control the looting, the fighting—in fact, some even volunteered to do so. But, reportedly, we said, no, thank you, and kicked them out the door.

It makes me wonder what would happen if some other random country came in and fired all the U.S. Military, security, and intelligence officials in one fell swoop? First, the unemployed would get angry. Second, they would look to organize—because that's what militaries do. Third, they would find some motivating and inspiring leader to coalesce behind to reclaim their pride, honor, and homeland. And that's exactly what the Iraqis did—against Western forces, a.k.a. the United States. It really doesn't feel like it should have been difficult to foresee this scenario, even with the benefit of hindsight.

Sometimes, as a country, we really suck, despite our good intentions. We make poor decisions around the world. And then we wonder why countries aren't more grateful for our "help" or why it feels like we are stuck in endless wars.

CHAPTER 16:

Good Days

Working in Baghdad wasn't all doom and gloom, bombs and bullets. I loved my coworkers. And occasionally, my job brought me a real sense of pride and feelings of accomplishment, along with the heartache. Three weeks after I arrived, an email came into the generic American Citizen Services information account and found its way to me. It was from a mother, who also happened to be a retired criminal investigator for the U.S. Marshals Service. Her son, who had been working in Baghdad for a private contracting company, had been killed by a car bomb four months earlier. For four months, this grieving mother had been contacting her son's employer, the FBI, and the Department of Defense, but had been unsuccessful in her attempts to gather information on what happened to her son and his convoy, let alone identify a case agent assigned to investigate the bombing. Something that was obviously important to her grieving process. Her outreach to the American Citizen Services Office felt like grasping at straws, a final attempt to make contact with an actual person who could get her the answers she desperately needed. Again, there was no script for handling these types of situations in the Consular handbook. Diplomats don't usually serve in warzones.

I responded to her email stating,

My name is Amy Lenk and I am the American Citizen Services Officer at Embassy Baghdad. Let me first just say that I am sorry for your loss and that I may not have all the information you are looking for—but I would be happy to help coordinate your efforts and try to assist in any way that I can. At this point I am not sure what information is available. Based on your email, it sounds like you would like additional information on the investigation that took place after the incident. I can't make any promises, but if you could send me information on who've you contacted, what/if anything you've been able to ascertain at this point, and a list of your specific questions, I'll see what I can do.

Grasping at the lifeline I threw her, the mother responded immediately with the scant details she had been able to gather and the runaround she had been put through by her son's company, the FBI, and the Department of Defense. As he worked for a contracting company and not the Department of Defense directly, her search for answers seemed to be caught in an endless finger-pointing loop. By doggedly hounding a couple of military offices, I tracked down some additional information. I'm not sure how much it helped in the end, but I think she was grateful nonetheless.

Given that Consular sections around the world issue visas and are generally involved in the creation and filing of vital documents, they are heavily guided by strict rules and regulations, and rightly so. I soon found, however, like with my attempts to help a grieving mother, I took the most joy in helping people navigate through the bureaucracy to ease the burdens of a warzone, even if only in a small way. One of my American coworkers and I went out of our way to help the especially desperate soldiers who needed passports. As I mentioned, the military would send soldiers to Baghdad equipped with only their military IDs. The problem with that was, in order to take their R&R (rest and relaxation) outside of the United States, they had to have a passport. We'd have guys who literally spent days trying to catch various rides, from the frontlines somewhere, to the Green Zone because they needed a passport for a vacation that started yesterday. They'd show up in our Consular waiting room, still covered in the dirt and grime of the desert, desperation written all over their faces. They had no forms filled out. No passport photos. And they had no idea what was necessary to be issued a passport; they were just told to go to our office to get one. When one of these especially young, fraught, frontline soldiers showed up at our interview window, we would bend the rules just a bit. Instead of sending them back across the Green Zone, to the PX, to get official passport photos taken, and waste yet another day, we used our own cameras and took their pictures ourselves and then printed them out on our printer. We helped them fill out their forms and expedited the processing of their applications in our system. The simple gratitude that washed across their faces, when they expected to be met with mounds of bureaucracy and paperwork, always brightened our day.

The same colleague and I also helped create our own ritual to honor the fallen. There was no guidance on how we, as an embassy or as State Department employees, should mourn the loss of American life in Iraq, in fact the subject was rarely talked about. But we felt compelled to do so nonetheless. As mentioned, the consular section was in the official U.S. Embassy building (not the Republican Palace where most government offices were housed). As such, and shortly after I arrived in Iraq, I met an Air Force 1st Lieutenant who told me that he and his boss were going to find their way to the roof to fly flags over the embassy on September 11 to take home with them. Inspired by his action, and when faced with grieving friends of the dead, my coworker and I would on occasion offer to briefly fly an American flag (purchased from the PX) over the embassy in remembrance of the deceased. After taking it down, we used our computers to make homemade, but official-looking, certificates that said something along the lines of, "This American flag was flown over the U.S. Embassy in Baghdad *on such and such a date* in honor of [insert name of deceased individual] soldier for their brave service to the

United States." We were never told we could do it but we were also never told we couldn't—so, we just did it. By honoring the dead in our own small way, it felt like we were reminding the living soldiers that their lives mattered as well and that they had a purpose beyond themselves.

One of my favorite days in Baghdad by far however, was the day I got to restore citizenship to a proud American. There was a Brigadier General in the Iraqi military who befriended a U.S. soldier; war zones have a way of bonding individuals to each other with atypical strength and rapidity. This U.S. soldier brought the General to our offices, as the General believed he might be eligible for American citizenship, based on the time he'd lived in America as a child. Perusing his provided documents and photographs, and after consulting the citizenship and naturalization acquisition charts, I agreed. Gathering his documentary evidence and signed statements, I sent the package of materials off to Washington, DC and waited.

Apparently, my decision stood. The powers that be in Washington agreed that he was indeed an American citizen. It was the first (and only) time I actually got to affirm someone's U.S. citizenship, and I was so touched by the soldier and General's friendship, that I wanted to do something special to mark the occasion. It sounds super cheesy, but I printed out an 8×10 copy of a U.S. flag on my color printer and tacked it to my cubicle wall with little gold thumbtacks. (When I think back on this story, I wonder why I didn't just run over to the PX and buy an actual flag. There must have been a reason.) I called the U.S. soldier and had him bring the General to our office. I asked the General to stand next to the paper flag and put his hand over his heart and repeat the oath of citizenship after me. I then handed him his passport and we had a small party in his honor in our office. I'll never forget that single tear that rolled down the proud General's face as he repeated his oath of citizenship.

Some months later, I received a call from a Regional Security Officer asking if I had indeed restored the General's citizenship (and that his pass-part wasn't some forgery). I confirmed that I had done so. Apparently, the General was applying for a job as a security guard at a Las Vegas casino and had to undergo a background check. The casino wanted to confirm that he was legit. It felt like a far way to fall, from General to casino guard; but a price I believe he was willing to pay for a chance to start his life over in a safer, more secure country.

CHAPTER 17:

Days That Sucked

Along with the good, satisfying days, inevitably came the bad. And there are some faces from those bad day that I'll never forget.

In one case, an American citizen came to see me. He acquired U.S. citizenship at birth as one or both of his parents attended college in the United States. After his parents graduated college, the family returned to Iraq, never to set foot in America again. This gentleman had no ties and no family in the United States. He did not speak English. His family in Iraq had been killed, he was alone, he was penniless, and he wanted out. He was hoping that the U.S. Government could buy him a plane ticket to somewhere, anywhere in the United States. In government lingo, it's called repatriation.

Side Note: In limited circumstances, the U.S. Government may be able to loan citizens money necessary to return home, in case, for example they are robbed of their possessions while traveling abroad and have no friends or family that can wire them money.

The problem was that the citizen standing before me had no location for me to repatriate him to. Despite having lived in the United States for one or two years as a baby, he had no U.S. address. And no family or friends with a U.S. address. I literally had nowhere to send him. I had to break the news that unfortunately I could not pay for him to go to the United States, but that he was welcome to present himself to a U.S. border agent with his American passport anytime, at any U.S. port of entry. He started crying. This big, burly, proud Iraqi man was openly sobbing with tears of desperation. He could not afford a plane ticket. On top of that, he feared that the insurgents had learned of his citizenship and that he would be targeted and killed. I'm not sure if he was truly afraid of death, or said so in hopes that it would make his case stronger. Regardless, at the end of the day, I was bound by bureaucratic rules. I had to send him away from the U.S. Embassy—still crying—I felt completely helpless.

Another example actually happened twice, like some horrible déjà vu. I listened to almost the same depressingly sad story two times, practically word for word. They both went something like this—an Iraqi woman came to my interview window, crying. She said I had to help her son (or daughter) who was American. I asked for more information. She showed me wedding certificates and pictures and other relevant documentation, and went on to tell her story of falling in love with an American contractor, who was kind and considerate. They were so in love, apparently, that the American converted and became a Muslim so they could marry. Shortly after the happy nuptials, she became pregnant. However, soon after that, his contract was up and he had to return to the United States.

Amidst his tearful departure, the husband admitted that he was already married, with children, in the United States. So unfortunately, he couldn't take his new pregnant bride home with him. And, U.S. law did not recognize the marriage to the Iraqi woman, as it was a second marriage. Polygamy is illegal under U.S. law.

Therefore, the Iraqi-born child could only obtain U.S. citizenship and move to the United States if the father was willing to attest to his parentage and support said minor. On both occasions, I reached out to the alleged fathers. On one occasion, the father responded. And for a while, both the Iraqi woman and I thought the father was actually going to follow-through and recognize his child. Ultimately, he didn't. On the second occasion, I never even received a response to my initial inquiry or follow-up messages. Looking into the pleading, desperate eyes of a mother and telling her, "I'm sorry but I have tried repeatedly to contact the father but have gotten no response. I cannot grant your child U.S. citizenship," was beyond words. Especially when the mothers both broke down sobbing, saying I just handed them and their children death sentences.

For both Iraqi women, they were married under the laws of their country and single mothers, with no husband to help support or protect them. They were also likely being ostracized by their families and living in a warzone. All I could do was say, "I'm so terribly sorry," and turn and walk away.

I don't even know how to write about my absolute worst day in Baghdad. It started with a morning phone call from my dear friend Carrie and three simple words she blurted out before I could even say hello. "Kevin is dead," she said. "What?" I automatically responded, hearing her, but unable to process what she was saying. "Kevin is dead," she repeated more forcefully. For several moments, silence hung heavy in the air between us, my mind racing with questions and things to say, but not sure how to say or ask them. "What do you say to a dear friend, upon learning her husband was just killed in Iraq?" I asked myself. My tongue was paralyzed, I was in shock, and it felt like I'd just taken a punch to the gut.

Kevin couldn't be dead. It didn't make sense. The world still needed him. My friend and her little boy still needed him.

Kevin defied expectations for me. A small-town southern boy who entered the U.S. Army straight out of high school, he was one of the most intellectually curious people I knew. A history buff and keen to understand politics and international relations, our conversations took us to unexpected places. I was convinced he'd go far in the Army. He had a gift for applying strategy and tactics in a most thoughtful and considerate way. He also had a fascination with bombs and was part of the Army's Explosive Ordnance Disposal (EOD) unit. He was on his third tour to Iraq.

Breaking the silence, Carrie said, "They're not telling me the details. I need to know how he died. Can you find out what happened?"

As if her request made it OK for me to talk again, my tongue started moving and I said, "I'm so sorry. But yes, I'll find out what happened," not really sure how I was going to accomplish that, but certain I would.

We hung up and I immediately called Joe who had good connections with the military in Baghdad, thinking, "He might know who I can talk to or where I can start to get answers about Kevin." Without hesitation, he said he knew a couple of guys we could talk to and that I should meet him in front of the Republican Palace. In a frenzied shock, I rushed to our rendezvous point, and together, we burst into a small military office in the Palace. As we entered, two men in uniform slowly turned away from their computers and looked at us expectantly, curious at our abrupt intrusion.

Trying to maintain composure while standing there, but failing, through my tears I looked at them and said, "My dear friend just called me. Her husband, who is an Army EOD soldier was killed somewhere in Iraq. The liaison officer didn't give her any details and she wants to know how he died." Armed with only his name, which I provided, one of the officers swiveled his chair back to his computer and began typing. Finding an incident report, he turned back around and said, "Don't worry—your friend will get the answers she needs."

Thanking him, we left the office. My task done; I could no longer distract myself with "helping." I was left with nothing but my thoughts and a deep sense of sadness.

Soon after, Carrie called again. Her assigned liaison officer had called and said, "I just got a call from a Colonel in Baghdad who told me I needed to get you more information. I'm doing the best I can, I'm trying to figure out what happened. I don't know who your friend is, but can you just tell her that I'm trying really hard?"

I was thankful I had done what I could; the details did start to come in. Called in to assist, Kevin had successfully disabled a roadside bomb. He was killed when searching for a potential secondary explosive device. It is believed that the insurgents who planted the explosives watched him dismantle one bomb safely. Before he could do the same with bomb number two, they set it off and he was not wearing a blast suit. Apparently, the suits get too hot in Iraq and make it harder to take bombs apart. My friend was told that protective gear would not have made a difference for Kevin anyway. He was practically standing on top of the bomb when it was set off. No suit would have been able to save him.

As if that wasn't bad enough, months after Kevin was buried, my friend received a call from the Army. They said, "We found more pieces of Kevin. What would you like us to do with them?"

I have no words to describe the awfulness of such a call. My friend once said if not for her young son's needs, she would not have been able to get out of bed in the morning those first few months.

CHAPTER 18:

At Least I'm Not in the Military...

On days that really, truly, horribly sucked in Iraq, I'd seek solace in the thought that my life could be worse, much worse. I imagined a list of things in my head that could make my life harder or more depressing. I'd think, "My husband didn't die. I'm not an Iraqi who's lived through multiple wars. I'm not in the U.S. Military..."

Even after living among soldiers for months, I still felt like the Defense Department was a completely different culture and one that as a civilian, I could never hope to completely understand. Looking in from the outside and comparing myself to women in the military, I felt like being in the State Department gave me a *get out of rape free* card. While never firsthand, I heard many stories of military sexual assaults endured by female soldiers in Iraq, in addition to the horror of being on the frontlines. I never heard similar stories from U.S. civilian women in Iraq. Not to say none of them were ever raped, but if they were, it wasn't frequent enough to become common knowledge.

As I mentioned earlier, having an entire shipping container to myself and a shared bathroom with only one other woman was living the life of luxury compared to Defense Department employees who had to bunk together and walk to separate bathroom trailers. There were many reports of military women being raped, by fellow American soldiers, while simply trying to walk to the bathroom at night. I can't even imagine the trauma. Here they were fighting for the freedom of our country, and they couldn't even safely brush their teeth. It is beyond infuriating. The fact that military sexual assault is still a thing we have to worry about is incomprehensible to me.

One of my hula and belly-dancing military friends told me about a young female soldier just out of high school and boot camp, who fell in love with another soldier. She was eighteen and in Iraq with the military. Despite the horrors of going to Iraq, her boyfriend made her feel safe. And even though General Order #1 said she wasn't supposed to have sex with him, she decided to anyway because "they loved each other." And that bastard, without the young girl's permission, recorded their sex with a hidden video camera. After showing her the recording, he said, "You have to either sleep with me and all my buddies or I'll turn this in and you will be discharged from the military for disobeying General Order #1."

Just like that, her life came crashing down. Her boyfriend didn't love her, he'd used her. And she acquiesced to his demands and slept with him and all his buddies. I think it's easy from the outside to judge her and think, "Didn't she realize that if she broke General Order #1, then so did he? And would he really have turned in the recording because it could have potentially implicated him as well?" The point is, she felt powerless. She was risking her life for all Americans and felt powerless, not because of some external foreign combatant that threatened her but because a fellow American soldier, someone she thought loved her, threatened her and then gang raped her.

It was after that story that I made a promise and vowed, "If I ever have daughters, unless military culture does a 180, I will never, ever let them become soldiers." Sometimes when walking around the Green Zone, I couldn't help but wonder how many of the men in uniform I saw were rapists. Considering the statistics on the number of male and female soldiers who experience military sexual assault, either a lot of soldiers are rapists, or a few men are sure raping *a lot* of people. It reminded me of being in Germany in the 1990s, and an American friend telling me that every time she saw a man in his seventies or older, she couldn't help but wonder if he had been a Nazi.

While I could fill an entire book with stories of sexual assault in Baghdad, which I heard second-and third-hand, they are not mine to tell. But I can't help from telling just one more.

While I typically drove to and from work, on some nice, winter days, when the heat wasn't too repressive, my colleagues and I occasionally walked. We would often pass the Green Zone hospital. On one of those days, a male colleague decided to walk home from work. The next day, he, part horrified and part traumatized, confided that as he was passing the hospital, a prepubescent, lanky Iraqi boy, who presumably lived in the Green Zone, approached him. This boy was likely ten to twelve years old. The boy offered him a blow job in the alleyway next to the hospital in exchange for twenty-five dollars. Staring at the boy, he politely turned him down and continued his walk home.

Upon hearing about this, my first thought was, "That kid wouldn't make that kind of offer unless some men were taking him up on it." It made me sick to my stomach to think there were guys letting a young Iraqi boy give them a blowjob for twenty-five dollars.

After retelling the story of my colleague's sad encounter to everyone I knew, a well-meaning man tried to explain that war often brings out the worst in people. He said, "When the world feels like it's on the brink of destruction, men have a biological need to spread their seed and perpetuate the species, so they become more sexually aggressive. As a woman, you can't really understand this because in times of war, a woman's sex drive diminishes. Women biologically understand that a war zone is not a safe place to raise a baby. And women instinctually crave the safety of a nest in order to procreate."

All I could think was, "You've got to be fucking kidding me! That's supposed to be a justification for child abuse? For rape? For abusing positions of power? For all the horrible tales I've heard? Because, biologically, a warzone makes men want to spread their seed!? It's called freewill buddy! Have you heard of it? It's what supposedly separates us from animals, makes us better, more advanced. Use it and walk away now, asshole. Just walk away. Quickly. Before my animal instinct starts unleashing some of my fury on you. I'll show you how I feel safe in my nest."

CHAPTER 19:

Runaway American Teenager

On one of my more mundane days of processing passport applications (it was the holiday season and the office was pretty much deserted), I received a call from a Baghdad-based AP reporter who said, "Did you realize that there is a sixteen-year-old American kid here at our hotel? And he's been walking around outside by himself." The reporter was not in the Green Zone. He was in the middle of the car-bombing, bullet-flying, terrorist-ridden Red Zone, where insurgents made money by kidnapping and selling foreigners.

I responded with a very professional, "No, no I did not know that. Thank you so much for calling. I would appreciate any additional details that you might have." The reporter went on to say that apparently this kid showed up in Baghdad with the audacious goal of walking around the streets of the city to interview locals about their feelings about the war and its aftermath. It was for his high-school journalism class—in Florida. His parents were Iraqi immigrants, but he didn't even speak Arabic. For the purposes of this story, I'm going to call him JJ (short for junior journalist).

After begging the reporter to refrain from publishing an article about JJ until after I could arrange to get him safely out of the country (he was a walking hostage risk or worse), I worked with the AP and the military to coordinate JJ's pickup and delivery from the embattled Red Zone to the relatively safer Green Zone. I met the military convoy that had gone to the hotel to pick him up in the PX parking lot, where he was handed off into my care. One of the soldiers gave me a half-smirk as he helped JJ off the Humvee and asked, "Are you the one looking for this kid? Good luck."

Shielding my eyes against the bright, Baghdad sun, I looked up at the soldier and responded with a simple, "Yep, that would be me," inwardly hoping I could resolve the situation as quickly as possible and get JJ's butt back on a plane to the United States.

The first thing I did was take JJ back to my office to call his parents. They were not living together, so he had to make two separate phone calls. He pleaded with me not to call them. I said, "I'm sorry, we have no choice. You're a minor. We have to let your parents know what's going on." Both conversations were pretty short. After identifying myself and briefly explaining the situation, in both instances, I handed the phone to JJ, so he could assure his parents he was safe and would be returning to the United States soon.

I then took him to lunch, where he told me more about his high-school journalism project and his desire to understand how Iraqi citizens felt about the war and subsequent occupation. I told him that I understood and commended his desire to learn more, but traveling to a war zone alone, as a sixteen-year-old was really dangerous—life and death kind of dangerous. And that it might not be the best way to get the information he was looking for. I could tell my warnings were not getting through to him. It felt like everything I said fell on deaf ears, he had the impetuous sense of immortality that comes with youth. Based on our conversation, I thought even if I get

JJ on a plane out of Baghdad, there's a good possibility, he'll just return the next chance he gets.

Again, there is no playbook for Consular Officers on how to babysit runaway American teenagers in a war zone. Rightly or wrongly, I thought maybe I could scare some sense into him and prevent him from cavalierly walking into a war zone again in the future. I pulled out my cell phone and called my buddy at the Hostage Rescue Team (HRT), and said, "I'm here with a sixteen-year-old American who traveled on his own to the Red Zone to learn more about the situation on the ground for Iraqis. I was just wondering if you have a few minutes to give him a quick briefing on what you see and do?" Without me saying so, he caught on that what I was really asking was, "Can you *scare the shit* out of this kid, so he doesn't come back? I don't want him to become one of your future cases."

I'm not sure if JJ realized what I was doing. He was just excited. As a student of journalism, he was getting more access than he had even hoped for. He was going into the Republican Palace to get a private briefing from an official who was responsible for rescuing American hostages in Iraq.

My colleague and I both tried. He talked about his job and painted a pretty grim picture of what can happen, has happened to hostages in Iraq, including gruesome details. But nothing seemed to faze this kid. I gave up trying to get through to him and instead just focused on getting JJ home.

He had a return ticket for a flight out of Baghdad's commercial airport a day or so after he'd arrived in the Green Zone. And initially, I thought we could safely transport him to the airport and quietly send him home on his original, commercial flight. After our day of phone calls, and lunches and briefings with officials, I drove him over to the Green Zone hotel. After he checked in for the night, and before he headed up to his room, I told him to stay at the hotel until I returned the next day to pick him up. I was concerned he'd run back to the Red Zone, so I thought it best he stick with me, as much as possible. Once he was out of sight, I turned to the concierge, gave him my number, and said, "Please call me if you see him trying to leave the hotel." Crossing my fingers that JJ would be in the lobby the next morning, I headed home, thinking I could get him home without too much additional effort, beyond a little babysitting. Then the media broke the story, a day earlier than hoped. The AP apologized to me. Other media outlets had caught wind of the story and they didn't want to be scooped.

I was understandably pissed. While I appreciate the role of the media, I felt like in this instance, they were putting a minor American's life at risk and causing me more work. Since his name and photo were splashed across newspapers and some of the articles mentioned that he came from a privileged background, Dick and I decided it was no longer safe for JJ to fly out on his commercial flight. JJ's risk of becoming a hostage victim had gone up too high. There was a good chance someone might recognize him at the commercial airport. I had to make alternative arrangements to get him home.

Setting all my other Consular duties aside, I spent the day on the phone. A friend was already planning to take the Rhino to the airport that evening and leave Baghdad via a military flight to Kuwait or Jordan, before making his way home via a European layover. After asking him to pretty please serve as an escort to JJ, I pulled a few strings with some Defense Department folks I knew to allow JJ a seat on the same military transport plane. I owed them big time. As a civilian without military ID, technically JJ should not have been allowed on the military flight. But I begged, making the case that it was necessary to save this kid's life. No one wanted blood on their hands if he was taken hostage from the commercial airport. I took him to the Rhino that evening and waved as he boarded and was sped off to the military side of the Baghdad airport, escort by his side. Breathing a sigh of relief, I thought, "Thank God, he is out of here." I wasn't quite ready to celebrate completely though, there were still a couple of legs to his trip before he was back on American soil.

My friend took JJ as far as Amsterdam; from there he boarded a commercial flight home. I got the call that they made it to Amsterdam and that JJ was at his gate while I was in the middle of a holiday party in Baghdad. Stepping away from the festivities, I called his mother and was momentarily confused by her over-effusive response to his imminent arrival. All of our previous conversations had been brisk, to the point, and emotionless; the comfortable place from which I prefer to operate. During the course of the call, it became clear that the media was in her house and listening to what we were saying. Not comfortable with being part of a spectacle, I hung up as quickly as possible.

Upon his arrival home, JJ participated in a press conference where he thanked the military for getting him home safely.

My first petty thought was, "Wait…the military? I get that they provided the actual transportation, but where's the love for the State Department? I arranged for your safe transport to the Green Zone, your meals, your flight, your calls to your parents, your hotel…?" My second thought was, "He's sixteen, forget about it. He's giving the people what they want to hear."

My job done, I breathed a bigger sigh of relief, and got back to celebrating the New Year—2006 had arrived.

A year or two later, I read a newspaper clipping about JJ showing up unannounced and touring Afghanistan. I never compared notes with the Consular Officer in Kabul, but I guess my scare tactics with the hostage briefing hadn't stuck.

CHAPTER 20:

Getting out of Iraq

My year in Baghdad quickly, but yet slowly behind me, it was time to fly onward to my next assignment. My third tour as a Foreign Service Officer was in Dubai in the United Arab Emirates as the first Economic Officer for the then, newly created, Iran Regional Presence Office (IRPO). It was recognized that because the United States had been run out of Tehran in late 1979, the State Department didn't have a dedicated field team of officers reporting on Iran. And since the State Department couldn't go to Tehran, Dubai, due to its proximity and its role as a major regional transportation hub, was the next best thing.

And so, after one intense year of gunfire, bureaucratic boredom interrupted by heartache and mayhem, and enough catcalls to last a lifetime—I finally got to leave. I definitely had survivor's guilt. It didn't feel fair that my time was up, that I had put in my one year, and that I got to simply walk away. While the Iraqis that I had learned to love had to stay behind. They did not have a one-year time limit. They could not just be done with the war and move on to the next country.

The first hurdle to leaving Baghdad was completing my "departure checklist." When Foreign Service Officers leave an overseas posting, there are numerous administrative tasks that must be attended to. Usually, these are things like turning in keys and forwarding mail, that sort of thing. Next to each task item on the departure checklist is a line that has to be initialed, confirming it was done. In addition to the standard checklist, I was required to make an appointment and meet with the on-staff psychiatrist. I spent all of two minutes talking to him about my next posting, when he abruptly said he was ready to sign off on my departure.

I said, "Wait, that's it?! That's all you need to know? Don't you need to delve into my brain or something to make sure I'm OK before you sign?"

"I could, if you really want me to," he said. "But I think you're good to go. I have a lot of people to see and I really only worry about those who want to stay in Baghdad. You clearly want to go, so I'm not worried about you. I can sign your sheet now."

"Oh…OK," I said, somewhat hesitantly, handing over my list for his initials.

I walked out of his office thinking that the psych checkout didn't feel quite thorough enough. I knew I'd built up a lot of baggage over the past year, shoving emotions deep down, vowing to "deal with them later." But, I kind of understood his point. I had met many warzone junkies in Baghdad, the diplomats or contractors or journalists unable to adjust to life outside a war or conflict zone anymore, and so they extended their tours or bounced from danger to danger posting.

I once met a diplomat who came to Dubai for a weekend vacation; he was on his third consecutive danger posting. He was literally shaking with excess adrenaline or anxiety or something when a group of us tried to take him out for a typical night on the town in Dubai, a little drinking, a little rooftop dancing. Worried on his behalf, I wondered how the State Department could continue to send him to dangerous posts, absent a psychological intervention. Anyone who bothered to take a look at the guy for more than a minute could clearly see he was not OK. I think there was a policy on the books about not doing multiple danger postings in a row, but if there was, it wasn't always enforced. The political realities dictated that diplomats were needed across multiple warzones. And it was likely more appealing for HR to send willing volunteers, as opposed to taking someone away from their family, to send them to Basra or Mosul or Herat.

After packing up my trailer, primarily clothing, a few souvenirs, and a couple of books to be sent ahead separately, and giving the rest of my stuff away to my coworkers, it was time to go. I took one last look around my Baghdad trailer, making sure I didn't forget anything. Surprised that I felt a little nostalgic for another chapter coming to an end, I got my gear together— backpack, check; flak jacket, check; helmet, check. Gear in hand I made my way to the designated Rhino assembly point, well past my bedtime.

At the Rhino bus depot, I was faced with the option of sitting outside on the pavement or in the indoor waiting room, I couldn't decide which one was better—or rather worse. The outside option offered a not-so-enticing hard, expansive parking lot with loose little sharp pebbles that dug into my skin, leaving my thighs and behind red and pockmarked even through my chinos. Whereas the waiting room had those annoyingly bright fluorescent lights that give me a headache plus uncomfortable, molded plastic chairs. To top it off, the room wasn't all that big and there were enough bodies, wearing lots of gear, to give it a slightly pungent smell. With an expected wait time of one to five hours, neither option was appealing. Because smartphones were not ubiquitous then, I had no gaming apps to keep me occupied. So, I bounced back and forth between the two, staying in one place until I couldn't stand it any longer before moving back to the other.

Eventually, we were hustled into the Rhino and sped the 7.5 miles to the airport in silence. I felt like talking would have been an interruption of the solemnness or might somehow jinx the ride. Not talking felt right.

Stepping off the Rhino on the U.S. Military side of Baghdad International Airport (BIAP), I made my way over to the large departure tent. It was the first stop in a long line of stops and designated assembly points that travelers were herded through on their way out of Iraq. On the several trips I'd made in and out of BIAP—my wait time varied between two hours (lucky) and eighteen hours (not so lucky).

Ducking through the tent door, I shrugged off my flak jacket and helmet, scanning for the designated PPE drop-off site. It was my last trip out of Baghdad and I no longer needed it for the flight I was scheduled to take. Rolling and stretching my shoulders, it felt good to be rid of the weight. I never did get used to the straps cutting into my shoulders. Probably because I ignored orders and didn't wear it, even when I was supposed to when driving around the Green Zone. Strapping on a flak jacket and helmet was heavy and uncomfortable, especially in a desert climate. Mine had gotten little use, except when I was forced to wear them by the military to ride on the Rhino or take a flight on a C-130.

Turning in my helmet and flak jacket, I got in line to confirm my request for a plane seat. Getting a seat on a plane was typically first come, first serve, unless someone of higher rank showed up and bumped you down the list—which had happened frequently enough to me, I was pretty low on the totem pole. Once my name was checked off, I began another wait in a designated assembly—again with the option of indoors or out. Every hour or two, they'd announce the names for the next plane's manifest. Every time I closed my eyes tightly and desperately waited for my name to be called, fingers crossed. Knowing this was my last trip out—I was so ready to leave.

On this final departure—on my way to Dubai and my new job—my BIAP wait time was closer to the eighteen-hour mark—the romantic part of me affectionately thought of it as a going-away present (a nice way of giving me the finger) after serving a one-year tour in Iraq. I actually found an email I composed to a friend, while waiting at the airport. It went something like this:

Arrived at BIAP during the night, was told I had an 1100 showtime for my flight out (*Note: this was after having been up all-night waiting for the Rhino departure from the Green Zone*).

At 1100, I was told to come back at 1230 for a departure briefing.

At 1230, we were told the plane was coming in at around 1300.

By 1400, we still had no word and were starting to get restless...then an announcement: our plane broke, but they were going to try and get us on another flight so we should stick around.

At 1500, we thought we were going to get on a plane at 1730.

At 1630, we were told to come back at 1900.

At 1930, we were told we could take the flight—but KBR would not support us on the other end...I said I was going to do it anyway...then I was told I needed PPE as it was a military flight, and of course I'd already turned mine in since I was leaving post. So, I begged, pleaded, and smiled at the Air Force guys and they scrounged an extra flak jacket and helmet. Then I was told a few minutes later I couldn't take the flight anyway as there were no seats left for civilians...still waiting.

If I'd known I was going to be waiting that long, I could have gotten a ride to the other side of the airport base where there was a building specifically for civilians to hang out and rest. But because I'd been repeatedly told my flight was on its way, there wasn't time to leave. I had to hang out at the tarmac, a.k.a. a dirt lot. The seats in the tent were all occupied, so I waited outside at a picnic table, strung-up camo netting was the only protection from the heat and glare of the sun.

When my name was finally called, I assembled, along with the others on my flight, in a third or fourth designated area (I lost count)—where yet another wait began. After the plane was ready to go—it always needed to be gassed-up and checked over before taking off, I walked single file, across the tarmac out to the C-130. I strapped into my jump seat and sat; willing the plane to take off and have my year in Baghdad behind me, but scared of it doing so all the same, at least until we were safely beyond Baghdad's airspace.

I don't recall when we actually took off, but I arrived in Kuwait (diplomats could choose to either fly to Jordan or Kuwait from Baghdad), and had to stay at the airport to catch my commercial flight to Dubai. Originally, I'd expected to be in Kuwait City long enough to stop by a KBR facility to sneak in a nap and a shower.

Side Note: KBR was a massive military contractor that took care of many things—including travel logistics. There were KBR houses we could stay at when traveling in and out of Kuwait, if layovers permitted. A major political scuttlebutt of the time was that between Dick Cheney's tenure as Secretary of Defense from 1989 to 1993 under President Bush, Sr. and his time as Vice President under President Bush, Jr., he was Chairman and Chief Executive Officer of Halliburton. KBR was a subsidiary of Halliburton and held one of the largest contracts given during the Iraq war called the Logistics Civil Augmentation Program (LOGCAP). LOGCAP was accused of hundreds of millions of dollars of fraud.

With no time for a shower and nap in Kuwait, I arrived in Dubai parched and dirty—like a nomad who had been wandering around the desert for days. In a nod to military-style cargo pants, but not quite willing to go there, I was wearing tan J. Crew straight leg chinos and a plain royal blue crew neck tee-shirt. Or maybe they were wearing me. I'd been traveling for an excruciating forty-eight hours, coming out of Baghdad. I was caked in layers upon layers of dry, dusty, desert dirt, and sweat. My fingernails were thick with grime, despite trying to unsuccessfully pick the dirt out. My hair was an uncontrollable frizzy mess, with wisps sticking up and out of my head. My eyes were bloodshot, my skin was sallow, probably owing to my slightly dehydrated state and my teeth desperately needed brushing—I think something was beginning to grow on them. In other words, I was gross—really, truly, horribly gross. And I'm sure I smelled a bit ripe too, despite the repeated swabs of deodorant under my arms every bathroom break I got.

I stumbled around the airport, looking everywhere, but not taking anything in. I felt overwhelmed, dazed, confused even. There were so many bright fluorescent lights. And stores stocked with merchandise. And people not in military uniform. And there were no guns. And talk about the food choices, there were too many to count. And the bathrooms were positively gleaming. "I must be in shock," I thought, if I think the Dubai airport bathrooms are A-MA-ZING. My senses couldn't take it all in. I remember the Emirati Border Control official giving me the twice over, skeptically studying my diplomatic passport for what seemed like a really long time. Normally a flash of my black diplomatic passport allowed me to breeze through customs. If the U.S. Consulate hadn't sent a local expediter to meet me, I don't know if they would have allowed me into the country. In fact, I'm pretty sure I would have been turned away or held for further questioning.

CHAPTER 21:

Adjusting to Dubai

Once I finally made it through the Dubai airport, a Consulate employee took me to my new home for the next two years, an apartment that was built on top of a shopping mall. I went down to the mall the day I arrived and walked around in a stupor. Similar to my experience at the airport, I couldn't focus. There was too much stimulation all at once. All of my senses felt like they were on overload. I quickly left.

My apartment, high above the mall, was thankfully a haven of tranquility. It had a beautiful view overlooking the Dubai Creek. And it was visually the most palatial and stunning apartment I'd ever lived in and probably ever would, it was a far cry from my Bagdad trailer. The reason I say "visually" is because, like many buildings of that time, it was built by Pakistani and Bangladeshi indentured servants at a speed likely not advisable for constructing multistory apartment complexes. I was one of the first tenants in the entire complex. Shortly after I got there, black mold began to appear on the ceilings of its three showers. I was told there was a problem with the air conditioning system, or maybe it was leaky pipes. I complained several times and each time they'd send a nice young man with a can of white paint who would paint over the black spots to make it look pretty again, and then he'd be on his way. Still, I didn't *want* to complain, I was living the life of luxury on the dime of American taxpayers. A perk for American Government employees working overseas is that housing is chosen by the State Department and paid for by U.S. taxpayers. This isn't the case in Washington, DC. When working at the State Department headquarters, there is no housing perk. But, as a part of their official job requirements, most diplomats are expected to entertain foreign officials in their homes (particularly higher-ranking diplomats). If I had been left to my own devices to find housing in Dubai on a U.S. Government salary, I would likely have ended up in a flophouse somewhere that would not only have compromised my physical security but could also have been embarrassing for the United States when I hosted various dinners or brunches.

The day after I arrived in Dubai, I went to the office to report for duty. Those first couple of days are a blur in my memory. I do vividly remember though the first time I met my new colleagues. Every time a Foreign Service Officer gets to a new post, it's like being the new kid in school. There's normal office drama stuff to learn, combined with that feeling of living in a small town—we all knew each other's business, and what wasn't known was filled in with gossip and conjecture. For instance, I was immediately told about the domestic abuser in Dubai. Everyone at the Consulate was pissed because his wife had recently been medically evacuated for injuries, yet he was still serving at post. My coworkers couldn't understand why the Ambassador hadn't kicked him out of the country yet.

By accident, I also found out about the affair a recently departed intern had with an officer. I was issued her old cell phone, complete with suggestive photos of her on a bed, saved to its memory. I never shared the pics with anyone (I *told* people about them, I just never *shared* them, which is how I learned about the affair). I deleted the pictures immediately, but that could have been really embarrassing for them had someone else received the phone.

On my first day, I walked up to a group of female officers who were chitchatting in a circle and thought about politely making my way into the group. But as I approached, I overheard one of them complaining about not being able to find a specific hair care product in Dubai. The first thought that went through my mind was, "You've got to be fucking kidding me! That's the extent of your problems? Dubai doesn't carry the exact hair care product you've been using all your life?" It was at that point, I just turned and walked away before introducing myself. I couldn't relate. My mind was still on bombs and bullets and war zones and insurgents and kidnapping victims. A lack of desired hair care products did not seem relevant.

For the first week or two, I walked around in a fog. At some point, I realized it would be better to be nice to my colleagues instead of ignoring them so I made up my mind to fake it until I make it. You know, pretend. I went to their weekly Project Runway television show viewing parties. I went dancing. I tried to care about others and their problems, even if seemingly inconsequential. But living in a war zone had changed me, their "problems" felt small. And I couldn't help feeling detached, like no one else got it, got me.

CHAPTER 22:

Numbers Have Faces

In terms of my work, my tour in Dubai was vastly different than Baghdad, although it also began with crying. Normally, I would not consider myself a crier. Most people would probably say I'm more aligned with the emotionless robot side of things. And I can be an awkward hugger too. I've been known to get confused and try to shake someone's hand when they are trying to go for a hug, and I end up giving them an uncomfortable pat on the back. We (my husband, children, and I) once had a French au pair who asked me if I was always so cold (she was talking about my personality). I get where she was coming from, but it still didn't feel nice. I spiked to a 5.6 on my emotional scale when she asked that—maybe.

I'm trying to learn how to show more emotion. I've been practicing. Every year, when my husband brings home his bonus check from work, I give a little jump, maybe a squeal, maybe an awesome, a congrats, a high five—whatever I can think of. Apparently, after twelve years, it still comes off a little stiff and rehearsed. It's a work in progress. I would be a horrible Wheel of Fortune contestant.

One of my many life mistakes was flying directly from my tour in Baghdad to my new position in Dubai, without taking a vacation in-between to decompress. Every couple of years spent overseas, State Department employees take "home leave" to reconnect with the United States and not forget where loyalties lie. I was supposed to take home leave after Baghdad, but somehow, I postponed it.

I was appointed to be the first Economic Officer to staff the new Iran Office (IRPO) in Dubai. And there was pressure by the home office in Washington to get the office up and running as quickly as possible. Not wanting to start off on the wrong foot, I hightailed to the United Arab Emirates, showing up at the office the day after I arrived in the country. I was the second IRPO staff member to get there (my boss was already there), and the one with the least knowledge of Iran, so I tagged along to various meetings, trying to get up to speed with all things Iran and its economy.

One of my first meetings was at a Dubai-based think tank, primarily staffed by Germans. It was located in a sparkling new skyscraper, worlds apart from my Baghdad lifestyle. My boss, the think tank head, and two of his employees were discussing the situation in Iraq. I sat there quietly, sitting back from the table, taking it all in, but not contributing.

At that point, it had only been a couple of weeks since I'd left Baghdad. My boyfriend of the time (someone I met in Baghdad) was still in Iraq. My friends and coworkers were all still there. Needless to say, a piece of my heart was still in Baghdad. And here we were, sitting around a glossy-wooden table in comfy over padded office chairs in a beautiful meeting room with an amazing view of the new, shiny Dubai skyline. We were served tea and delectable snacks, while the meeting participants discussed how many more Iraqi civilians needed to die before the world community would wake up and give a shit and intervene to a greater extent. I was not ready for the conversation—not at all. I had not put enough emotional distance between myself and Baghdad. I didn't trust myself to speak.

And then it happened. My boss turned to me. It was one of those moments where life slowed down and I desperately wished I could press the rewind button. My brain willed the words she was speaking to go back into her mouth. But that didn't happen. Instead, she said, "Amy just arrived here from Iraq after spending one year in Baghdad. Amy, do you have any thoughts or insights you would like to share?"

I know she was just trying to be nice and include me in the conversation, trying to give airtime to a more junior colleague. I should have said no, I really should have said no—but I didn't. I don't know why but I began talking. And the more I talked, the faster I talked. I could feel my heart palpitating, my eyes started to well up, my vision narrowed and the pitch of my voice went an octave higher. A year's worth of emotion just came spilling out. I started regurgitating the emotions and feelings that I'd bottled up for an entire year. I really should have insisted on that longer psych eval.

"My boyfriend is still in Iraq. My friends are still in Iraq. My coworkers are still in Iraq. And it saddens and frustrates me to hear conflict dehumanized to the point of calmly discussing the 'hundreds of thousands of innocent civilians that need to die,' before the world will give a shit and do something. To me, those numbers have faces," I said. "They have hopes. They have dreams. They are more than just a number; they are more than just a statistic. Those 'hundreds of thousands that need to die,' include people I love."

All eyes in the room were staring at me, slightly dumbfounded, unsure of what to say or how to say it. But still, I didn't stop. At that point, I couldn't stop. I continued, "I heard from my Iraqi coworkers that morgues are so filled beyond capacity right now with innocent victims, that bodies are piling up on the streets outside, rotting. Innocent people are being blown up in front them due to car bombs."

And then, thinking of all my friends who were still in Iraq and the danger they were still in, the fact that they were included in the "necessary deaths" to spur the international community to greater action, I began to cry. Deep, sobbing, whole-body shaking cries. And I couldn't stop. It was as if an entire year's worth of frustration and sadness and stress and fear was tumbling out all at once. That's when it got *really* uncomfortable in that pretty, shiny, fancy, sparkly Dubai office.

Representatives of the U.S. Government don't cry. Diplomats don't cry, at least not at work. They are always calm, composed, and professional. I can't think of a single occasion where I've ever seen a bureaucrat cry. Yell maybe, especially at the DMV, but not cry. Never cry. Not knowing what else to do, the head of the think tank awkwardly, but to my great relief at being spared additional embarrassment, looked at his watch and said, "Uhm, I think that's all time we have for today."

My boss and I quickly got up and left the conference room. That was it, meeting over. I walked out taking deep breaths, trying unsuccessfully to get the sobs to subside, willing the carpet to swallow me whole as all eyes in the office turned and stared at what felt like our slow-motion departure. I was beyond embarrassed.

Getting into the car, I managed to calm myself on the fifteen-minute drive back to the Consulate. And after we parked, and took the elevator back to our office, my boss tried to make me feel better about the whole situation. She said, "You know, Amy, I would rather have someone working for this office who is committed and passionate about the work they are doing to serve the country, as opposed to having someone who is indifferent."

It felt like she was placating me, but I appreciated the gesture, and knew she was doing her best to make an uncomfortable situation a little easier. She went onto recommend a therapist—a recommendation that I didn't even entertain, not for one second. I'm not sure what it's like now—but at the time, seeking out a therapist was a potential black mark. In fact, there was an unstated, yet understood belief that it could cost you your security clearance, which had to be renewed every five years. And not getting a security clearance renewed was a career killer, which was not a risk I was willing to take. I had big, ambitious plans for my Foreign Service career. I knew I needed to keep a stiff upper lip and just get my shit together. It was time to pull up my big girl pants and squash those emotions back down inside and get to work. Emotions could be dealt with later or, more likely, not at all. Diplomats don't cry. At least not while working.

About six months after the Dubai bawling incident, I attended a cocktail party at the same think tank. It was the first time I'd returned and I felt a little sheepish. One of the German women who had stone-faced witnessed my emotional outpouring approached me. She told me very calmly, very matter-of-factly about a story she'd recently read in the newspaper. Apparently, a number of Iraqi children had been blown up. They had died at the hands of a suicide bomber while lining up to receive teddy bears or candy bars from some foreign troops. After relaying the horrific story, she said, "Reading the story made me think of our meeting with you. I understand why you cried." There was a pregnant pause as we both awkwardly looked at one another, neither of us knowing what else to say. And then she turned and walked away.

EPILOGUE:

My Life Post-State

During my second year in Dubai, I went on a two-week scuba diving and sailing trip from Thailand to Malaysia with a small tour company. I didn't know anyone else who was going, but I signed up anyway as it sounded fun. By day three, one of my fellow trip participants and I knew we were meant to get married—which we did, several months later. I did mention that I like to make major life-changing decisions rashly.

He had just accepted a new job in the San Francisco Bay area and I had one year left in Dubai. We hatched some crazy scheme to maintain a long-distance relationship for one year, taking turns to fly to each other's location until we could figure out our next step. As we knew we wanted to spend the rest of our lives together, we wanted the rest of our lives to start as soon as possible and thought we could figure out the details along the way.

Then I got pregnant on our honeymoon. And I didn't want to be pregnant with our first child and on my own in Dubai. I tried to get the State Department to approve an extended leave without pay for me, but I wasn't able to bend the bureaucracy to fit my needs. So, I quit the Foreign Service. My husband's new job paid much more than my government salary and therefore seemed like a better fit to start a family.

Quitting my job and moving to San Francisco, where I didn't know anyone except my husband, threw me into a huge identity crisis. Visibly pregnant, at that point, I was convinced I wouldn't be able to find a fulfilling job. I did a little part-time nonprofit consulting, but going from a diplomat who had recently been in charge of a presidential visit in Dubai, to a stay-at-home pregnant wife, felt surreal. Competitive and ambitious, I'd had big plans for my State Department career. On more than one occasion, a senior member of the Foreign Service had told me that I would be an Ambassador one day, to which I would sassily respond, "At least."

A photo of the president and me in early 2008.

For years I was a little resentful that my husband got to keep his job and have his wife and kids, while I had to trade a fulfilling career for a fulfilling personal life. I'd try to snap out of my funk by sternly telling myself, "You need to get over yourself. By having a place to live, a husband who loves you, and money in the bank, you are better off than most people in the world. Who cares if you don't feel intellectually stimulated? Stop your whining already. You're smart. You'll find your way. Just relax. So many people would *love* to be in your position."

Working through my identity crisis, and having three kids in three years meant I could put off dealing with the emotions I squashed while in Baghdad.

It took me a long time, a decade even, before I could even admit that living in Iraq had impacted me. My experiences didn't seem to warrant the sadness I felt, and shouldn't make me cry. I wasn't in the military. I never had to go to the frontlines and shoot people. I was never raped in Baghdad, like so many serving in our armed forces. I didn't know what it was like to have to work with colleagues who had attacked me or exist in a system that completely failed me. I had spent one year, protected, in Baghdad's Green Zone. My experiences never felt like enough to justify post-traumatic stress.

And so, for a long time, I pretended. I pretended to relate. I pretended to miss people when they were gone. I pretended to care about things, even when I couldn't bring myself to.

And, I think I'm finally getting better. I have friends I care about. I love my three kids individually, if not collectively (collectively their whining and bickering sometimes drives me nuts). I genuinely miss my husband when he's at work or traveling. And I'm doing a pretty good job about getting excited when he brings home his bonus check. Well, at least I think I am.

ACKNOWLEDGMENTS

First, I would like to thank my dear friend Amanda White. She painstakingly read through a very rough first draft of this book. Her edits and insights helped me find my voice. Also instrumental were my sister Melissa Lenk and journalist Tamara Bralo. Their excitement to read the chapters, as I finished them, and to provide helpful feedback was the encouragement I needed as I worked through drafts two and three. And to my other readers who let me know that they found the book enjoyable, I thank you. You helped me believe in myself and the possibility of this book.

I would be remiss if I did not thank my family for their unending patience. On more than one occasion, when interrupted by one of my kids, tears streaming down my face as I poured my heart and soul into this book, I went straight to yelling, "GO! GO! Just GO! Get out of here! Shut the door! Mommy's in the middle of her book. I need to finish this thought."

Finally, I would like to thank the authors who took the time to describe the traditional publishing world to me. Because of their experiences, I decided to self-publish with the support of online publishing services. And so, to all of the anonymous editors and designers that helped me with this book, thank you.